HOW TO DRAFT EASEMENTS

DEAN N. ALTERMAN

ABA
AMERICAN BAR ASSOCIATION
Real Property, Trust and Estate Law Section

Cover design by Andrew Alcala

Printed in the United States of America.

25 24 23 22 21 5 4 3 2 1

Library of Congress Cataloging-in-Publication Data

Names: Alterman, Dean N., author.
Title: How to draft easements / Dean N. Alterman.
Description: Chicago : American Bar Association, 2021. | Includes index. | Summary: “A book to help you write easement agreements clearly and effectively, not just for your clients but for the ages”—Provided by publisher.
Identifiers: LCCN 2021019225 (print) | LCCN 2021019226 (ebook) | ISBN 9781641059725 (board) | ISBN 9781641059732 (ebook)
Subjects: LCSH: Servitudes—United States.
Classification: LCC KF657.A75 2021 (print) | LCC KF657 (ebook) | DDC 346.7304/35—dc23
LC record available at https://lccn.loc.gov/2021019225
LC ebook record available at https://lccn.loc.gov/2021019226

Discounts are available for books ordered in bulk. Special consideration is given to state bars, CLE programs, and other bar-related organizations. Inquire at Book Publishing, ABA Publishing, American Bar Association, 321 N. Clark Street, Chicago, Illinois 60654-7598.

www.shopABA.org

Contents

About the Author

Dean Alterman is the founder and president of Alterman Law Group PC, a real estate and business law boutique firm in Portland, Oregon. A graduate of Harvard College and Lewis & Clark Law School, Mr. Alterman has practiced real estate and business law in Oregon since 1989. His varied career includes eight years as a real estate agent, five years as a director of a community bank, and three years as chair of a county planning commission. He is admitted to practice in Oregon and Washington.

In the thirty-three years since the American Bar Association published his first article on a real estate topic in its journal *Probate & Property,* Mr. Alterman's writing on real estate law has appeared in professional publications, in general media, and on his firm's website, www.alterman.law. In 2015, the American Bar Association published his first book, *How to Build a Real Estate Law Practice*.

Introduction

Thank you for reading my book on easements. I know that you're only at page xi. I'm an incurable optimist and am expressing my appreciation in advance.

This book is not a textbook, nor an academic paper, nor a fifty-state survey of the condition of easement law. I've entitled it *How to Draft Easements*, but I hope that you will read this book as more than a collection of forms. This book does have a collection of forms in the back, and most of the chapters include sample clauses indented and set off in a different typeface, like this:

> 5. Grantor reserves the right to use the Easement Area for any purpose that does not conflict with Grantee's use of its easement rights, including but not limited to building and using nonresidential structures that extend to no more than X feet above ground level and that maintain at least Y feet of clearance between the top of the structures and the lowest powered wire on Grantee's poles.

Not all of the indented clauses are ones that I recommend that you use for your own agreements. In some sections I start with a poor clause, explain why it misses the mark, and then give a series of suggestions on how to improve it, adding to the clause with each suggestion.

Easement agreements are some of the most curious inhabitants of the real estate world. In the thirty-plus years since I drafted my first easement agreement, I've sometimes pondered how their brevity contrasts with their longevity. Compare easement agreements to deeds, mortgages, and leases. A deed is a very short document, one or two pages plus exhibits. Except for the seller's warranties of title, when the deed is delivered and recorded its job is done. A lease may run for twenty, forty, or sixty pages to define a relationship that may last for only ten years.

An easement agreement may be only a few pages long—much shorter than most commercial leases—and yet it defines a relationship that, except in North Dakota, may last forever. (Current North Dakota law limits easements to a term of ninety-nine years.) When you draft an access easement over a neighbor's property for your client, you are writing an agreement not just between your client and the neighbor, but between the future owners of the two properties. You are writing a contract that will bind and benefit people whom neither you nor the actual parties to the easement agreement will ever meet.

I don't mean to get metaphysical here, but to encourage you to focus on the practical consideration that if a dispute about the easement agreement comes up ninety years from now, the people who own the two parcels won't be able to ask the parties or the drafter what they meant. I hope that my book will help you write easement agreements clearly and effectively, not just for your clients, but for the ages.

1
What Is an Easement?

1.1 The Classical Definition

What is an easement? The classical definition of an easement is a nonpossessory interest in the land of another that entitles the holder to use the land for a particular purpose. These words, or words very much like them, appear in statutes and judicial opinions on the law of easements.

For example, someone building a skyscraper who needs to use a tower crane to lift materials may ask a neighbor to grant a crane swing easement to allow the contractor to swing the crane boom above the grantor's adjoining property. The builder is using the neighbor's land (actually, the neighbor's airspace), but is not possessing it.

The grantor may give the grantee not only the right to use the grantor's land for that purpose but also the right to alter the land or build permanent improvements to carry out the grantee's purpose. For example, the grantor of an access easement may give the grantee not only the right to cross the grantor's property to get to and from the grantee's property, but also the right to build and maintain a driveway on the grantor's property. The grantee is not taking possession of any part of the grantor's property, as the grantor may use the driveway also.

1.2 Easements and Licenses

Easements and licenses both give the grantee the right to use the grantor's property for a particular purpose. The two important distinctions between an easement and a license are (a) the grantor may revoke a license at will, but may not revoke or terminate an easement unless the grantor has reserved that right in the easement agreement; and (b) an easement appurtenant runs with the land and benefits future owners of the grantee's tract, but a license is personal to the grantee and does not pass to later owners of the grantee's tract.

A client who wants to grant a right to a neighbor that the client may revoke at will may ask you to draft an easement agreement to grant that right. Explain the differences between an easement and a license and ask if what the client really has in mind is to grant a revocable license, and not a permanent easement. If the client wants to grant a right to the current neighbor but not to any future owners, offer to draft a license agreement. If the client wants to grant a right to the current neighbor and to future owners, you can prepare an easement agreement with a clause that allows the grantor to terminate the easement.

1.3 Easements and Profits à Prendre

Easements and profits à prendre both give the holder the right to use the land of another. The traditional distinction is that the holder of a profit à prendre may remove property from the grantor's land for the holder's own use and benefit. (*Prendre* is a French verb that means "to take.") Hunting and fishing rights can be profits à prendre because they include not just the right to enter the grantor's land to hunt or fish but also to take away the animals that the holder catches. Rights to harvest timber or mine gravel can also be profits à prendre. The holder may enter the grantor's land and remove timber or gravel for the holder's own benefit.

1.4 Easements Expand Beyond the Classical Definition

The classical definition is a good starting point. It is not complete. Lawyers create nonpossessory interests in land that are not easements.

Lawyers create documents called "easements" that do not entitle the holder to use the land for a particular purpose. Lawyers even create documents that give the holder the right to possess the land of another and sometimes call those documents "easements." The easement tent has grown since the days of Blackstone.

Some grantees get exclusive rights—the right to be not only the only holder of an easement, but the right to be the only one to use the facility in the easement. The grantee of a pipeline easement acquires not only the right to enter the grantor's land to construct the pipeline, but also the exclusive right to use the pipeline.[1] A pipeline easement includes the right not only to enter to install and maintain the pipeline but also often the exclusive right to use portions of the land that will have pumps or other facilities. It's hard to think of the pipeline company's interest in the land as entirely nonpossessory when it acquires the exclusive right to use a portion of the land and the pipeline that it intends to build.

The grantor of a landscaping easement, sometimes called "the poor person's lot line adjustment," usually grants an exclusive right to the neighbor to landscape and use the area on the neighbor's side of the misplaced fence, even to the exclusion of the property owner. Even though we entitle the document as an "easement agreement," it's granting the neighbor what for all practical purposes is a permanent possessory interest in a portion of the grantor's property. Chapter 9 covers landscaping easements that substitute for property line adjustments.

Consider the owner of a downhill property who promises the uphill neighbor not to build anything on the portion of the downhill property where a building would block the uphill neighbor's view. A century ago, lawyers would have called the agreement a "negative covenant" or a "restrictive covenant." Today we would title the agreement a view easement, even though it does not fit the classical definition of an easement. The downhill owner is not giving the uphill owner any right to use the downhill property for a particular

[1] Imagine how an oil pipeline company will react when a farmer through whose farm the pipeline runs telephones with the news that the farmer wants to run water through the pipeline next Saturday to irrigate the back forty acres.

purpose, but only the right to restrict how the downhill owner uses the property. I discuss view easements in chapter 8.

1.5 Easement Agreements Can Last a Very Long Time

Many of the agreements that we write as lawyers aren't permanent. Most of a real estate sale agreement lasts until the sale is closed, with the warranties sometimes surviving a few years longer. A partnership agreement lasts for the life of the partnership, which may be many years, or just a few months. We even write some agreements that will be meaningful for only a few weeks. They "strut and fret their hour upon the stage / And then are heard no more."[2]

Not so an easement agreement. Some easement agreements create relationships that the parties intend to last only a few months; for example, an easement to swing a construction crane over adjoining property. Most easement agreements create relationships that the parties want to last indefinitely, that is, forever, or until the easement itself becomes obsolete a century or two later. Keep in mind when you draft an easement agreement that a hundred years later the owners of the properties tied to the agreement may dispute what it means, when the original parties will not be available to explain what they meant. Draft carefully and exactly for the benefit of the future reader; neither "marble nor the gilded monuments of princes"[3] may outlive the rights and obligations that your easement agreement is creating.

---

[2] Macbeth, Act V, scene 5, W. Shakespeare, lightly edited to fit the sentence.
[3] Sonnet 55, W. Shakespeare.

2
Basic Easement Theory

2.1 A Note on Terminology

In this book I am using certain terms to have an exact meaning.

An "easement agreement" is an agreement that creates an easement. An easement agreement can be an agreement between two parties, or a unilateral grant of an easement by a property owner to a grantee, or a declaration or reservation in a deed of real property.

An "easement" is the right that the easement agreement gives the grantee to use the grantor's property. I use "easement agreement" to mean the written document that creates or conveys the right to the grantee, and "easement" to mean the right itself.

An easement encumbers a particular piece of property: the "servient estate," "burdened property," or "burdened tenement." Your choice of term depends on your writing style and your law school's Property professor. The main distinction in easements is whether they benefit a particular property: the "dominant estate," the "benefited property," or the "benefited tenement," again depending on your preference.[1]

[1] A "tenement" is a building or other improvement on land. Long ago easement jurists applied the word indiscriminately to land and buildings, using "burdened tenement" to mean land subject to an easement, whether or not the land was improved. E.g., Richard Brooke Michell, *The Law of Easements, Natural Rights Arising from Situation, and Licenses, in India* (1898), at 109–110. "Tenements" are more popular to burden than to benefit. A Google search for "burdened tenement" gives 287 hits; one for "benefited tenement" returns only 123 hits.

In most of my examples I use the following terms. Read the sample clauses with the idea in mind that the following capitalized terms, if not defined in the sample clause, were defined in other parts of the easement agreement:

- "Grantor" is the party who is granting the easement via the easement agreement.
- "Grantee" is the party to whom the Grantor is conveying the easement. Usually, but not always, the Grantee will be a party to the easement agreement.
- "Grantor Tract" is the property that the Grantor owns, at least a portion of which is subject to the easement. The obligations of the easement agreement may flow with title to the Grantor Tract even though the easement itself affects only a portion of the Grantor Tract.
- "Easement Area" is the portion of the Grantor Tract that the easement agreement gives the Grantee the right to use.
- "Grantee Tract," in easement agreements that create appurtenant easements, is the tract that the Grantee owns that is to get the use of the Easement Area and the benefit of the easement agreement.

Every easement that an easement agreement creates is either an "easement in gross" or an "appurtenant easement." Easements in gross are for the benefit of a particular user but not for a particular piece of property. Appurtenant easements are for the benefit of a particular property, and the benefit of the easement passes with title to the benefited property.

2.2 Easements in Gross Benefit a User, Not a Property

An easement in gross burdens a particular property, or portion of a particular property, but is for the benefit of a particular user rather than for the benefit of the owner of a particular adjoining or nearby property. Its essential elements are:

- A grantor
- A grantee

- A burdened tract or portion of a tract
- A purpose or allowed use

The most common easements in gross are those for utility companies. An electric company that wants to build a transmission line from Hooterville to Pixley will acquire easements to cross the many parcels of private land in between. These easements aren't for the benefit of any particular parcel—the electric company will use the line to serve many customers—and they don't automatically pass to the buyer of any particular parcel that the electric company may own. They are easements in gross.

Railroads acquired many portions of their rights-of-way as easements in gross, and sometimes by documents that did not clearly state whether the grantor was conveying a fee title or an easement right. The unclear drafting of a century ago spawns litigation today.[2]

Newer flavors of easements in gross include conservation easements, discussed further in section 3.3, as well as easements for cell phone towers and facilities, and highway slope easements.

British common law did not recognize easements in gross as easements. As recently as 1868, a British jurist wrote in a railway case that "There can be no easement properly so called unless there be both a servient and a dominant tenement *** There can be no such thing according to our law, or according to the civil law, as what I may term an easement in gross."[3] America was more

---

[2] E.g., BNSF Railway Company v. Chevron MidContinent, L.P., Case No. 08-16-00119-CV (Texas Court of Appeals, 8th District, issued March 22, 2017), in which a railroad and an oil company argued whether a 1903 deed to the railroad granted the railroad merely an easement (Chevron's position) or the fee title, including mineral rights (BNSF's position). The deed described a strip of land as a "railway right of way" and granted the railroad "the privilege of taking and using all of the wood, water, stone, timber and other materials" on the strip of land that it might use to build and maintain the railway, which sounds like easement language. The deed concluded, however, with a broad habendum clause: "To have and to hold the said premises *** in fee simple."

[3] Rangeley v. Midland Railway Company, L.R. Ch. App. 306 (1868). See also G. Kloek, *Assignability and Divisibility of Easements in Gross*, 22 CHICAGO-KENT L. REV. 239, 241 (1944); L. Simes, *The Assignability of Easements in Gross in American Law*, 22 MICH. L. REV. 521, 522 (1924). Professor Simes states that "the English courts do recognize some easements in gross, but refuse to call them

flexible: easements in gross have been debated in our courts since at least 1858.[4]

One quirk of English common law that did survive to plague our courts is that in England, an easement in gross was personal to the grantee and did not pass to the grantee's heirs and assigns—it died with the grantee. The English reasoning was set out in *Ackroyd v. Smith* in 1850 and came to be known as the Ackroyd rule.[5] The English courts reasoned that because an easement in gross did not benefit any particular tract of land, it did not pass with the land. Because an easement in gross benefited a particular person for some presumed private purpose of the grantee, the grantee's purpose would die with the grantee.

What made sense (barely) for grants between individuals in the English countryside became obsolete when railroads, wires, and pipelines began to span cities, states, and the continent. American courts that felt constrained by the Ackroyd rule would stretch their logic to find that challenged easements, in gross on their face, were in fact appurtenant to some other property, and did not die with their grantees.

In the United States, the Ackroyd rule is fading, but it is not gone, and it still crops up from time to time in state court opinions. Some states have rejected the Ackroyd rule entirely and have allowed easements in gross to be assignable. Others have excepted commercial easements in gross (principally easements for railroads and utility networks) from the Ackroyd rule and have held that those easements are assignable. At least one state now considers the intent of the grantor and grantee: in 1999, the Maine supreme court held that an easement in gross could be assigned if the parties intended that it be assignable.[6]

---

by that name," and cites Lord Cairns's statement, though he misdates it as 1808 instead of 1868.

4 Garrison v. Rudd, 19 Ill. 558 (1858). Another early case involving an easement in gross is Boatman v. Lasley, 23 Ohio St. 614 (1873).

5 Ackroyd v. Smith, 138 Eng. Rep. 68 (Court of Common Pleas, 1850). An attorney for American Telephone & Telegraph Co. described the history and misapplication of the Ackroyd rule in 1945, arguing that American courts should simply set it aside as a relic of a bygone era. Gerald E. Welsh, *The Assignability of Easements in Gross*, 12 U. Chi. L. Rev. 238 (1945).

6 O'Donovan v. McIntosh, 728 A.2d 681 (Me. 1999). A good discussion of the history of the Ackroyd rule in Maine and elsewhere is found in Michael J. Polak, *O'Donovan v. McIntosh: Changing the Contours of Maine's Easement Law*, 52 Me. L. Rev. 447 (2018).

Even in the states where it survives, the Ackroyd rule is of little practical concern to owners of property encumbered by railroad and utility easements. Few people want to litigate against a railroad or utility company to argue that an easement through their property was not assignable and therefore terminated when the local power company merged into another. Americans are, however, creating hundreds of new easements in gross that are not to railroads and utility companies and are not for the purpose of creating a service network. These are conservation easements, discussed in section 3.3 in chapter 3, and are easements in gross to a nonprofit organization that restrict development of the encumbered property, for which the grantor commonly claims a substantial income tax deduction. If a nonprofit organization that holds conservation easements in an Ackroyd-rule state should dissolve, do the conservation easements terminate because the dissolving nonprofit cannot assign the easements to another nonprofit? Look for test cases to appear in the next few decades.

2.3 Appurtenant Easements Benefit a Particular Property or Small Group of Properties

Appurtenant easements (historically often called easements appurtenant) are for the benefit of a particular property. Unless specifically excepted from a deed, they pass with the title to that property and will benefit future owners of the benefited property. When a seller conveys the benefited tract to a buyer, the seller automatically conveys the appurtenant easement with the property.

Compared to an easement in gross, an appurtenant easement has one additional element, which is that it must benefit some identified or identifiable property that the grantee owns. The essential elements of an appurtenant easement are:

- A grantor
- A grantee
- A burdened tract or portion of a tract, owned by the grantor
- A benefited tract or portion of a tract,[7] owned by the grantee
- A purpose or allowed use

[7] An easement will usually burden only part of the grantor's tract. Only rarely, however, will an easement benefit just part of the grantee's tract instead of all of the tract.

The most common appurtenant easements are probably for access: driveways and walkways. Some utility easements are appurtenant easements, as when one neighbor grants another the right to install a sewer or power line through the grantor's property for the benefit of the grantee's property. Another common appurtenant easement is the encroachment easement, when a landowner grants a neighbor an easement to maintain an encroaching fence or building on the grantor's property, discussed in chapter 9. Recent decades have seen the growth of view easements and "no-build" easements, discussed in chapter 8, all of which are appurtenant to adjoining or nearby properties. Even if they are not classical easements because they don't convey a right to enter the grantor's tract for the benefit of the grantee's tract, they are easements that benefit specific properties and not the world at large, and are thus easements appurtenant to the identified benefited properties.

2.4 Easements That Might Go Either Way

I began this chapter with the precept that every easement is either an appurtenant easement or an easement in gross. Despite the efforts of generations of jurists and law professors to follow that principle, a few easements are not clearly within either category. In general, easements that are created by easement agreements will clearly be in one class or the other. Some easements are created or first identified by a reservation in a deed, and some of the deeds that create those easements can be interpreted in several ways. Consider the following language in a deed that conveys a tract of land that lies near, but not on, Black Acre Road:

> Subject to a perpetual right of access to and from Black Acre Road on and across the existing private road on the above-described property as currently located and used.

How are we to interpret this provision? Here are three alternatives that future plaintiffs and defendants might argue to a court:

- The deed creates an easement appurtenant to (for the benefit of) nearby property that the grantor owns, allowing the grantor and all future owners of the grantor's property to use the existing private road to get to and from Black Acre Road.

- The deed excepts (is given "subject to") an existing right for the benefit of all users of the private road to get to and from Black Acre Road, and is appurtenant to all the land that now adjoins the private road.
- The deed reserves or attempts to create an easement for the benefit of whoever might want to use the private road to get to and from Black Acre Road, which is not appurtenant to any particular tract and is therefore an easement in gross.

The chapters that follow will explain how to draft easement agreements to reduce the chance that your clients find themselves in court arguing about their rights. Litigation is a blunt and expensive tool with which to settle a dispute.

2.5 Easements Can Last Forever

As I mentioned in the introduction, easements last indefinitely. If the parties don't agree that a particular event terminates the easement, and if nothing else terminates the easement, then the easement that an easement agreement creates will last forever.

Several different events can terminate an easement. Even though this book is not a legal treatise, I'll describe some of the events that can terminate an easement. You should have these events in mind when you draft easement agreements.

2.5.1 Termination by Agreement

The parties to an easement agreement can terminate the agreement and any of the easements that the agreement created. The right to terminate appurtenant easements passes to future owners of the burdened parcel and the benefited parcel. Occasionally someone will create an easement to comply with a land use requirement or a condition of approval of a development application and the local government will require the creator to promise not to amend or terminate the easement without the government's approval, even though the government is not the grantee.

2.5.2 Termination by Condemnation

Eminent domain, like gravity, is the law. If the government condemns the fee title to property that is subject to an easement, the government may condemn the easement also. The easement agreement becomes moot if the government condemns all of the easements that the easement agreement created. The issue for the property owner and the easement holder is who should get how much of the compensation that the government is paying for the property.[8] The government will pay the fair value of the property and leave it up to the property owner and the easement holder to argue about how to divide the proceeds.

2.5.3 Termination by Abandonment

The holder of an easement can abandon the easement. Abandoning an easement is more than just not using the easement. To abandon the easement, the holder must take some action that affirmatively shows that the holder no longer wants to exercise the easement right and use the easement area. Each state has its own slightly different formulation of this principle. Tennessee's is representative: "It has been repeatedly held that a mere nonuser[9] will not amount to abandonment of an easement, but that there must be some positive showing of an intent to abandon."[10]

How might an easement holder show an intent to abandon an easement? If the easement holder has an easement to use a driveway to cross the Grantor Tract to get to the holder's garage, and the easement holder tears down the garage and replaces it with a different garage and a different driveway, a court could take the holder's conduct as evidence that the holder was abandoning the easement.

Abandonment has been a prominent issue in litigation over railroad easements and in particular with rails-to-trails programs. Abandoned rail lines make great trails for hikers and bicyclists. They are

---

[8] For example, the Right of Way Manual of the New Hampshire Department of Transportation (as updated June 20, 2011) states that "If easements are acquired in the taking the value of easement should be estimated. An allocation should be made between the property owner and each easement holder property rights." *Right of Way Manual* 43.

[9] "Nonuser" is what nonlawyers would call nonuse.

[10] Boyd v. Hunt, 102 Tenn. 495 (1899).

linear and gently graded. They are also often built on easements, with the underlying fee title held not by the railroad but by the adjoining landowner. The National Trails System Act, 16 USC § 1241 *et seq*., authorizes governments to convert unused rail lines to recreational trails as an interim use. As state and local rails-to-trails programs have worked to repurpose abandoned rail lines as trails, landowners have sued to block the trails on the ground that the easements to the railroad terminated when the railroad abandoned the line and removed the rails.[11] In *Preseault v. Interstate Commerce Commission*, 494 U.S. 1 (1986), the Supreme Court held that the National Trails System Act was not unconstitutional on its face, even if it worked a taking of property owners' reversionary interest in rail easements over their property, because the property owners had the remedy to seek compensation under the Tucker Act, 28 USC §1491(a)(1). A full discussion of the topic is beyond the scope of this section and requires its own book.[12]

2.5.4 Termination by Adverse Possession

A property owner can terminate an easement by adverse possession, similarly to acquiring title by adverse possession. To terminate an easement by adverse possession, the property owner must so interfere with the easement holder's rights without interruption for the period of adverse possession. In one such case, in 1954 the grantors sold part of their property to Nassau Farmers Market together with an access easement over part of the rest of their property to provide access to a road on the east side of their retained property. The Nassau property passed to Spiegel and the grantors' property passed to Ferraro.

Some time before 1958, the owner of the Ferraro tract built a chain link fence along the boundary line between the two parcels. The owner of the Ferraro tract leased the tract to Ernie's Auto Body in 1966. Ernie's installed two gates in the fence and held the only keys to the gates. Ernie's also installed lights and kept guard dogs behind

---

[11] Unlike ordinary abandonment of an easement, where the easement holder simply stops using the easement and takes some action that's inconsistent with the holder's easement rights, a railroad that wants to abandon a rail line actually files a formal petition to abandon the line with the Surface Transportation Board, a federal agency.

[12] By another author.

the fence that patrolled the easement area, and parked wrecked cars on the easement area. Between 1966 and 1982, when Spiegel filed suit to enforce the easement agreement, Spiegel and his predecessors had not driven a car across the easement area. The New York Court of Appeals (the state's highest court) held that because Ferraro's tenant had effectively blocked Spiegel from using the easement area for more than ten continuous years without objection, Spiegel had lost his easement right in 1976 when the statutory ten-year period of adverse possession ran.[13]

The *Spiegel* court carefully distinguished between easements that had been opened up and easements that had not yet been opened. In the court's view, until the easement holder starts to use the easement area, the acts of the burdened property owner won't start the clock ticking on a termination claim. The court's theory is that until the easement holder needs to use the easement, the holder has no reason to care what the burdened owner does. However, if the easement holder starts to use the easement (that is, opens the easement area for use) and then is interrupted for the statutory period by the owner of the burdened property, the owner of the burdened property can claim that the easement was terminated by adverse possession.[14]

2.5.5 Termination by Merger

An easement is the right of one person to use the land of another without possessing it. You can't give an easement to yourself because you already have the right to use your own land—you don't need your own permission to use your own land.

If you buy a tract that comes with an appurtenant easement to use part of the neighbor's property, and later on you buy the neighbor's property, then your easement over the neighbor's property terminates because your easement right to use the neighbor's property merges into the title that you've just acquired. This becomes inconvenient if you later sell the property that used to benefit from

[13] Spiegel v. Ferraro, 73 N.Y.2d 622 (1989).

[14] The alert reader will have noted that it was not the property owner, Ferraro, who blocked Spiegel from using the easement area, but Ferraro's tenant, Ernie's Body Shop. The court held that the tenant's acts could give rise to a claim of termination by adverse possession because the tenant was not making any claim against its landlord.

the easement and you don't properly revive the easement when you convey the property. It's also inconvenient if you convey what used to be the burdened property and you don't reserve an easement to benefit the property that you're keeping.

2.5.6 Termination by Destruction

An easement can terminate if the part of the burdened property that the easement covers is destroyed or damaged to the point that the easement holder cannot use it for the purpose of the easement. For example, if the owner of Blackacre grants the owner of Whiteacre an easement to maintain a painted sign on a wall of the building on Blackacre, and the Blackacre building is destroyed, then the easement terminates. (This kind of situation doesn't often happen.) More commonly, if the owner of Blackacre grants the owner of Whiteacre an easement to use a staircase or fire escape in the Blackacre building and the building is destroyed, the easement terminates.

This doctrine does not apply if the owner of Whiteacre has the right to rebuild the improvement, as for instance with a driveway easement. If the driveway is damaged or destroyed but the land is still in place, the owner of Whiteacre may repair and restore the driveway and resume using the easement area. However, if the driveway is near the ocean and erosion causes it to fall into the ocean, the easement will terminate.

If you're drafting an easement agreement for the benefited party to use part of an improvement on the burdened property, and if you don't want the easement right to terminate if the improvement is destroyed, then you should say so in the easement agreement.

3
Easements in Gross: Overhead and Underground Utilities; Conservation Easements

As with an easement appurtenant, an easement in gross burdens particular property. The difference between an easement appurtenant and an easement in gross is that an easement appurtenant benefits specific other property. An easement in gross does not benefit any particular property: there is no dominant estate or dominant tenement to which the easement will attach.

This chapter discusses what you should consider when you draft or review an easement in gross for the two most common situations in which you're likely to encounter them: easements for utility lines and conservation easements.

3.1 Easements in Gross for Utility Lines

3.1.1 Easements for Overhead Lines

Your client has been asked to grant an easement to allow the local power company or public utility district to build an overhead power line through your client's property—not just to serve adjacent or nearby property, but to be part of the power company's general network. The power company has sent you its standard form of easement agreement. What should you look for in the agreement, and what should you ask to change?

3.1.1.1 Specify the Location of the Easement Area

First, does the agreement specify where the utility company will build the line? I still see utility company forms that don't identify any particular location for the line, with a granting clause that reads like this one:

> 1. For valuable consideration, Grantor grants to Grantee a permanent easement to construct an overhead power line with supporting poles and guy wires through the Grantor Tract.

The problem comes when the grantor wants to sell the Grantor Tract, because the buyer can't tell what part of the Grantor Tract is free from the easement, especially if the power company has not yet built a line. A title insurance company will show this sort of easement as an exception to title and state that it cannot determine which part of the property the easement encumbers. The buyer of a farm may be willing to accept this uncertainty. The buyer of a development site will not.

Compare that vague granting clause to this one:

> 1. For valuable consideration, Grantor grants to Grantee a permanent easement to construct an overhead power line with supporting poles and guy wires within a 10-foot strip of land (the "Easement Area") through the Grantor Tract, legally described on the attached Exhibit B[1] and depicted on the attached Exhibit C.

The second granting clause makes it clear that only a specified portion of the Grantor Tract is subject to the easement. Unless the rest of the easement agreement restricts how the property owner may

---

[1] Exhibit B describes the Easement Area. I'm assuming that Exhibit A will be the legal description of the entire Grantor Tract. If you describe the Grantor Tract in the body of the easement agreement, then Exhibit A will be the legal description of the Easement Area and Exhibit B will be the map of the Easement Area.

use the rest of the Grantor Tract, the property owner may be content that the utility company has not acquired any rights in the rest of the property.

3.1.1.2 Describe the Improvements That the Grantee May Build

You can improve the granting clause by specifying what the utility may build. By the time the utility company approaches your client to buy an easement, the company's engineers will have a good idea of what the line will be and how it will be supported. They will probably have done preliminary drawings of the line and selected locations for the poles and guy wires. Ask the utility to share those drawings with you and your client, then limit the easement to what the utility intends to build.

> 1. For valuable consideration, Grantor grants to Grantee a permanent easement to construct an overhead power line with supporting poles and guy wires (the "Improvements") within a 10-foot strip of land (the "Easement Area") through the Grantor Tract, legally described on the attached Exhibit B and depicted on the attached Exhibit C.
>
> 2. The size and location of the Improvements are approximately depicted on the attached Exhibit D, and Grantee will construct the Improvements to comply with the following specifications:
>   a. Grantee may install up to X poles.
>   b. Each pole may be no more than Y feet in height.
>   c. Each pole may be supported by up to Z guy wires, extending no more than K feet from the base of the pole.
>   d. The power lines must be at least M feet above the ground at all points.

A sophisticated property owner may also ask to specify the voltage of the wires, or put some other limit on how the utility uses the easement area, to prevent the utility from replacing the poles for a basic distribution line with a taller, beefier line.

The power company must construct the lines to conform to the electrical code. The National Electrical Safety Code (NESC), published by the Institute of Electrical and Electronics Engineers, provides clearance standards for overhead and underground power lines, and has been adopted in some form by many states.[2] Before you advise your client to sign an easement agreement that states that the power company will build the lines "to code," ask the power company to identify the code-required clearances and discuss them with your client. Ask both what your client intends to do under the easement area, not just now but in the future, and consider horizontal clearances as well as vertical clearances. NESC Rule 234C requires that the neutral wire on an overhead line be at least 10.5 feet above an accessible portion of the top of a building, but only three feet above a nonaccessible portion.[3] The same rule requires a horizontal clearance of 4.5 feet between a building wall or accessible area (e.g., a balcony) and a neutral wire.

If the easement agreement does not prohibit your client from building underneath the future power line, and if your client may someday want to build underneath the power line, then negotiate for the power company to install the line higher than the minimum requirement. Your client is unlikely to want to build a house directly underneath a power line, but might want to build a barn, a garage, or a workshop where the power line will be. Plan ahead.

3.1.1.3 Protect the Grantor's Right to Use the Surface

When you review the easement agreement, consider how it allows the grantor (your client) as well as the grantee to use the surface. As a principle of easement law, the grantor of an easement may use the easement area for any purpose that does not conflict with the easement agreement or the easement holder's use of the easement right. Easement agreements commonly contain a generic clause to this effect, such as "Grantor may use the surface of the Easement Area for any purpose not inconsistent with the rights herein granted to the Grantee."

Your client may want or need more than this generic clause. If your client plans to build a driveway underneath the power line, you should reserve that right and not leave it up to implication. If your

---

[2] Ordinary wiring in and around buildings is covered by the National Electrical Code, published by a different organization.

[3] "Accessible" means that the area can be casually accessed, without a portable ladder, crane, or other equipment.

client plans to build a structure in the easement area—not a house, certainly, but perhaps a workshop or carport—state that in the easement agreement. For example, you could propose to add this clause:

> 5. Grantor reserves the right to use the Easement Area for any purpose that does not conflict with Grantee's use of its easement rights, including but not limited to building and using nonresidential structures that extend to no more than X feet above ground level and that maintain at least Y feet of clearance between the top of the structures and the lowest powered wire on Grantee's poles.

3.1.1.4 What Is the Grantee's Right of Access?

Including the overhanging crossarms, the power company's distribution or subtransmission line may use a strip of land only eight or ten feet wide. Guy wires may extend a few feet outside of that strip, or may be entirely within the strip. The utility company may need to use more than a ten-foot strip to install the power line, which you should cover by splitting the easement agreement into two separate grants. One grant is of a permanent easement for the facilities; the other grant is for a temporary construction easement that expires on a fixed date or at a certain time after the easement agreement is signed or recorded. If the utility wants a temporary construction easement over a wider area than what it needs for the power lines, you can propose this clause:

> 1. For valuable consideration, Grantor grants to Grantee (a) a permanent easement to construct, operate, maintain, and repair an overhead power line with supporting poles and guy wires (the "Improvements") within a 10-foot strip of land (the "Easement Area") through the Grantor Tract, legally described on the attached Exhibit B and depicted on the attached Exhibit C, and (b) a temporary construction easement over an area extending five feet on each side of the boundaries of the Easement Area (the "Temporary Construction Easement Area"), which Grantee may use for access when Grantee is installing the Improvements. Grantee's right to use the Temporary Construction Easement Area terminates two years after this Easement Agreement is recorded.

3.2 Let's Dig into Underground Utility Lines

Easements for underground utilities present some additional considerations. One difference is that not only power and communications wires but also sewer, water, and natural gas pipes can be placed underground. Another difference between overhead easements and underground easements is that everyone can see the poles and wires in an overhead easement. By contrast, within a few years after the utility installs an underground line or pipe, it may not be at all apparent to a casual observer or a prospective purchaser of the property that anything runs underground.

You and your client have both practical and legal considerations when you evaluate the utility company's form of easement agreement. Some of those considerations are similar to those for easements for overhead utility lines, except that you will look down instead of up. Looking down is harder.

For safety reasons, natural gas companies and oil pipeline companies mark and inspect their underground easements. (Compare the difference between what happens when your excavator severs a telephone line and a natural gas line to understand why.) The safety concerns are lower, but still high, for underground electric lines. They are much lower for telephone and cable television lines. The difference in safety and in risk shows in how the easement locations are marked.

A visible manhole may provide access to a storm or sanitary sewer line, and a small box or a vault cover may contain equipment for an underground power or communications easement. The manhole, box, or cover may be the only indication that a power, telephone, or cable line is a few feet underground. If your client's property is not a tract of acreage it's possible that when the utility company has installed its line and the landscaping has grown back, there will be no trace at the surface that a line runs beneath the property.

3.2.1 How Low Must the Grantee Go?

The first practical consideration for your client is how far below ground the utility intends to place the line or pipe. Once a house has been built on a lot, we don't much excavate the surface below a foot or two, the depth to which we might dig to install lawn sprinklers or replace trees and plants—until the day we start to build a pool, or do major changes to the landscaping, or dig a hole for the foundation of an addition to our house. Our clients who may want to add on to their houses or construct an in-ground swimming pool need to know where the underground lines are, not only to avoid cutting a wire or breaking a pipe, but to avoid building an expensive improvement on top of the wire or pipe that the utility company might have to remove to repair a break. Be exact about the location of the underground line so that your client and future owners won't inadvertently build on top of an underground line.[4] Also specify a minimum depth for the underground line so that your client won't accidentally dig it up.

The granting clause in the easement agreement that the utility provides may read as follows:

> 1. For valuable consideration, Grantor grants to Grantee a permanent easement to lay down, maintain, repair, and replace an underground sanitary sewer line in the Easement Area.

Propose, instead, something like this clause:

> 1. For valuable consideration, Grantor grants to Grantee a permanent easement to lay down, maintain, repair, and replace an underground sanitary sewer line in the Easement Area, on the terms and conditions of this Agreement.
>
> 2. Grantee may install one underground sanitary sewer line within the Easement Area, the top of which must be no less than X feet beneath the ground surface as it now exists.

3.2.2 What Exactly Is the Easement Area?

You will have defined "Easement Area" to be the area that the utility company may use for its underground line or pipe. Read the company's proposed agreement carefully to determine whether the agreement imposes obligations on any of your client's property outside the easement area, or if it imposes an obligation on an area that can't be

[4] Some years ago, clients came to me because the gas company had just told them that they had built their new pool on top of an old easement and had asked them to remove the pool.

determined until after the company builds the line or pipe. Problems may arise if you aren't clear about the portions of the tract in which the grantee has rights. Here is an example of a problem caused by careless drafting.

In the 1930s, the Bonneville Power Administration (BPA) acquired a north-south easement to build high-voltage power lines through a farming area. In 1955, while the area was still agricultural, the gas company acquired an easement "over, across, and upon" the property west of the power line for the purpose of building an underground natural gas line. The recorded easement stated that the gas company would build the pipeline five feet from the BPA easement, and that no one would be allowed to construct any building within ten feet of the pipeline.

In the 1980s, development arrived and the agricultural property was subdivided. Prospective homeowners bought one of the lots west of the power line, through which the gas company's pipeline ran, and hired a homebuilder to build a house for them. The homebuilder had the property surveyed. The survey quite properly showed that the pipeline was on the building lot, five feet west of its eastern boundary line. The survey did not identify the easement area as being fifteen feet wide, but showed the location of the pipeline with the notation "Location of Pipeline per Book 377, Pages 74 and 76, easement width indeterminate." In fact, nothing in the easement itself directly stated that the easement area was of any particular width.

The homebuilder built the house less than ten feet from the pipeline. On a routine inspection, the gas company noticed the new house and asked the homeowners to remove the portion of the house that was within ten feet of the pipeline. The homeowners, not wanting to remove part of their house, sued the builder, the surveyor, and the title insurance company that had insured their purchase.[5]

Poor drafting was one cause of this lawsuit. The 1955 easement agreement did not define any particular easement area, but gave the gas company the right to build a pipeline in a specified location, and

[5] Womer v. Melody Woods Homes Corporation, 165 Or App 554, 997 P.2d 873 (2000). In earlier stages of the case, the author was one of the attorneys that represented the title insurance company.

then imposed a separate no-build obligation on a strip of the property that was referenced by the pipeline rather than by the boundaries of the property.

Imagine that we could go back to 1955 and assist the gas company in drafting its easement agreement. Instead of describing the easement grant as something like:

> 2. Grantor grants to Grantee and its successors an easement over, across, and upon the Grantor Tract for the purpose of constructing and maintaining a natural gas pipeline, to be located five feet from the western edge of that certain easement granted to Bonneville Power Administration * * *
>
> 3. No building shall be built within ten (10) feet of the location of the pipeline.

We could have advised the gas company to draft those clauses as follows:

> 2. Grantor grants to Grantee and its successors an easement over, across, and upon the east 15 feet of the Grantor Tract (that 15-foot strip hereinafter the "Easement Area") for the purpose of constructing and maintaining a natural gas pipeline, to be located five feet from the western edge of that certain easement granted to Bonneville Power Administration * * *
>
> 3. Grantor will not build any buildings within the 15-foot Easement Area.

If the gas company had drafted the easement agreement in this fashion, then any reader of the easement agreement would have understood that the gas company had the right not only to build a pipeline near the east boundary of the property, but also to prevent the property owner from building anything on the east fifteen feet of the property so that any future improvements would be at least ten feet west of the pipeline.

3.2.3 Surface Tension: What Must the Grantee Restore?

When the power company installs an overhead line, its facilities are plainly visible but often it doesn't disturb the surface very much.

The utility that installs an underground line usually must dig a trench through your client's property. The utility places the line or pipe inside the trench and then backfills the trench to the surface. In digging the trench, the utility of necessity removes the trees, shrubs, lawns, and walkways above and near to the trench.

The utility will want your client to promise not to build structures or plant deep-rooted trees in the easement area because they would make it more expensive to repair the line. In exchange for your client promising not to plant big trees or place expensive improvements in the easement area, the utility should promise to restore and relandscape the surface both after it places the underground line or pipe and if it should have to dig to repair it. Here are clauses that you can use as starting points to impose that obligation on the utility.

> 3. The Easement Area is currently landscaped with grass, shrubs, a walkway, and an underground sprinkler system.[6] When Grantee has installed its [underground pipeline] [conduit and underground wire] [Facilities],[7] Grantee will replace Grantor's landscaping in and around the Easement Area to have substantially its present appearance.[8]
>
> 4. If in the course of maintaining, repairing, or replacing the [underground pipeline] [conduit and underground wire] [Facilities] Grantee disturbs the ground surface, Grantee will promptly restore or replace any landscaping of Grantor that Grantee disturbed and restore the surface of the Easement Area to substantially its former appearance.

Be prepared for the utility company to object to having to replace mortared brick walkways and concrete flatwork.

---

[6] Adjust your description of the improvements as appropriate.

[7] You may have listed in another paragraph what the utility company can build and then defined that list as "Facilities." If so, use the defined term here.

[8] When it's time for the utility company to replace the landscaping, its memory of the landscaping may have faded. Consider attaching some photographs of current conditions as exhibits to the easement agreement.

3.3 Conservation Easements for the General Good

A conservation easement is an agreement in which a property owner promises not to develop all or part of a tract and identifies a unit of government or a nonprofit organization as the beneficiary of the easement.

3.3.1 Two Bodies of Law Control Conservation Easements

If your client is thinking about granting a conservation easement to the government or to a nonprofit organization, you have two bodies of law to keep in mind when you are negotiating the conservation easement. The first body of law is state law, which governs the creation and interpretation of easement agreements. The second body of law is federal tax law. Some landowners who grant conservation easements are motivated by a desire to preserve their property intact for future generations to enjoy but not develop. Others recognize the income tax benefits that they will receive from donating a conservation easement. A lawyer who competently crafts a conservation easement agreement that complies with state law but that misses some of the requirements to qualify the gift for a federal income tax deduction will have an unhappy client.

3.3.1.1 State Laws and the Uniform Conservation Easement Act

Start with your state law requirements. In 1981, the National Conference of Commissioners on Uniform State Laws proposed a Uniform Conservation Easement Act (UCEA), most recently revised in 2007. It was reported in 2014 that twenty-eight states and the District of Columbia had adopted some form of the UCEA, twenty-two states had adopted an enabling statute not based on the UCEA, and only North Dakota had not adopted any law to enable conservation easements.[9]

Conservation easements are often more like negative covenants (promises not to do something) than classical easements, because they don't have to give the grantee any right to enter and use the

---

[9] Robert H. Levin, A Guided Tour of the Conservation Easement Enabling Statutes (Land Trust Alliance 2010; updated 2014). Retrieved from landforgood.org/wp-content/uploads/CLE_Conservation-Enabling-Statutes-Guided-Tour-.pdf, March 2021.

grantor's property. The drafters of the UCEA explained that they had chosen to describe the interests of the grantees as "easements" because in their words:

> First, lawyers and courts are most comfortable with easements and easement doctrine, less so with restrictive covenants and equitable servitudes, and can be expected to experience severe confusion if the Act opts for a hybrid fourth interest. Second, the easement is the basic less-than-fee interest at common law; the restrictive covenant and the equitable servitude appeared only because of then-current, but now outdated, limitations of easement doctrine. Finally, non-possessory interests satisfying the requirements of covenant real or equitable servitude doctrine will invariably meet the Act's less demanding requirements as "easements." Hence, the Act's easement orientation should not prove prejudicial to instruments drafted as real covenants or equitable servitudes, although the converse would not be true.[10]

An easement qualifies as a conservation easement under the UCEA if it meets three basic requirements. First, the easement must grant to a "holder" a nonpossessory interest in real property that imposes limitations or affirmative obligations on the landowner to keep or protect natural, scenic, or open-space values of real property to assure that the property remains available for "agricultural, forest, recreational, or open-space use," or "protecting natural resources, maintaining or enhancing air or water quality, or preserving the historical, architectural, archaeological, or cultural aspects" of the property. Second, the holder of the easement must be (a) a unit of government that is authorized to own interests in real property, or (b) a charity that has the purpose or power of protecting those uses or values. (The American Red Cross would not qualify as a grantee because, although it's authorized to own real estate, its primary purposes don't include protecting open space

---

[10] Prefatory Note, Uniform Conservation Easement Act, 2007 revision, at 1–2.

and natural resources.) Third, the grantee must accept the conveyance and the easement agreement must be recorded.

The easement agreement may grant a third party the right to enforce the easement agreement if the third party is eligible to be a "holder," that is, the third party is a unit of government or a qualified charity. Under the UCEA, the conservation easement is perpetual unless the agreement limits its duration.

It's straightforward to meet these requirements if your state has adopted some form of the UCEA. Confirm that the grantee of the conservation easement is a unit of government that may hold property interests or a charity that includes preserving open space, natural resources, or architectural resources among its purposes. Next, describe the easement right that the donor is giving to the government or the charity. If your client owns 100 acres of farmed land and twenty-five acres of woodland and is donating a conservation easement over the woodland to a charity, your agreement could start like this:

> 1. Grantor hereby conveys to Grantee, as a gift without consideration, a conservation easement (the "Easement") over the 25-acre portion of the Grantor Tract (the "Conservation Easement Area") for the purpose of protecting the natural and scenic values of the Conservation Easement Area and assuring that the Conservation Easement Area remains available for forest, recreational, or open-space use, as further described in this Agreement.[11]
>
> 2. As part of the Easement, Grantor covenants not to use the Conservation Easement Area for any purpose other than forestry, agriculture, and outdoor recreation, and in particular not to build any enclosed structures in the Conservation Easement Area.[12]

---

[11] I recommend using words from your state's enabling legislation to describe the purpose of the conservation easement.

[12] You would write suitable language to describe what your grantor is agreeing not to do within the Conservation Easement Area, which will be different from my example. I did intentionally use the words "forestry, agriculture, and outdoor recreation" because they appear in the UCEA as allowed uses of the property.

3.3.1.2 The Internal Revenue Code and Conservation Easements

Some donors of conservation easements simply want to protect their property from later development. Others are motivated by the idea of obtaining a large charitable deduction. Sections 170(f)(3)(B) and 170(h) of the Internal Revenue Code allow donors of conservation easements to take a deduction for a charitable contribution on their federal income tax return, if the easement meets the requirements of the Internal Revenue Code. The Code's requirements are more stringent than those of the UCEA. Those requirements include:

- The easement must run in perpetuity—it must be permanent.
- The easement must be a true gift and not given in exchange for a zoning approval or other governmental permit.
- The grantor must not have reserved rights in the property that are inconsistent with the purpose of conservation.
- The easement must provide that if the conservation easement is terminated (as, for example, by condemnation of the underlying fee title), the charity that holds the easement must receive a proportionate share of the proceeds.
- Most importantly, the grantor must not overvalue the conservation easement.

Your client will rely on you to ensure that the client's conservation easement complies with the first four requirements. You will also want your client to commission a reliable appraisal of the value of the conservation easement, because when your client claims a large charitable deduction for donating the conservation easement, the Internal Revenue Service may want your client to explain how your client arrived at the claimed value, and to pay a large penalty if your client can't substantiate the claimed value or if the Service believes that the conservation easement does not meet all of the other requirements of the Internal Revenue Code.

3.3.1.3 Three of the Internal Revenue Service's Requirements Are Easy to Meet

Let's take those requirements in turn. First is that the easement must be permanent. This is a problem for would-be donors of interests in North Dakota property, because North Dakota has a unique law that limits the duration of easements to ninety-nine years and prohibits the grantor and grantee from agreeing on a longer period.[13] In 2014, the Tax Court held that because North Dakota law prohibits a conservation easement from lasting longer than ninety-nine years—that is, from being an easement in perpetuity—the donors of a conservation easement in North Dakota property could not take a charitable deduction for giving the easement to a conservation organization.[14] Until North Dakota adopts a statute that allows conservation easements to be perpetual, a would-be North Dakota donor of a conservation easement will not be eligible to take a federal income tax deduction for donating a conservation easement.

Even if the easement agreement is permanent, the restriction on the land must be permanent also. The donor of a conservation easement who reserved the right to substitute land near the easement area for land inside the easement area—that is, to move the easement area around after the donation took effect—was denied a deduction for the contribution because the easement agreement did not assure that any particular portion of the land would remain subject to the easement in perpetuity.[15]

Second, the easement must be a gift and not an exaction in exchange for a development permit or other favor from the government. A developer cannot take a charitable deduction for giving a conservation easement over a portion of a tract in exchange for getting permission to develop the rest of the tract, any more than the developer can take a charitable deduction for dedicating to the public the streets in the subdivision.[16]

---

[13] N.D.C.C. § 47-05-02.1(2).

[14] Wachter v. Commissioner, 142 T.C. 140 (2014).

[15] Belk v. Commissioner, 140 T.C. 1 (2013), 105 T.C.M. (CCH) 1878 (2013), *aff'd* 774 F.3d 221 (4th Cir. 2014). The *Belk* decisions have been criticized as placing an out-and-out ban on substituting property subject to a conservation easement (Morgan Davis, *Belk v. Commissioner: Land Substitutions in Conservation Easements,* 48 Loyola L. A. L. Rev. 1193 (2015)), and later decisions on substituted property have distinguished *Belk*. *See, e.g.*, Pine Mountain Preserve LLLP v. Commissioner, No. 19-11795 (11th Cir. 2020), reversing the Tax Court's decision, T.C. Memo 2018-214.

[16] Even if the landowner does not give the conservation easement in exchange for a permit, if the landowner is making the gift for the landowner's own benefit, the Service will challenge the deduction. In Wendell Falls Development, LLC

Third, the landowner must not have reserved rights in the property that are inconsistent with the purpose of conserving the stated historic, cultural, or natural values of the property.

3.3.1.4 A Tax Trap Lurks for the Unwary in the Fourth Requirement

Fourth, the easement agreement must provide that if the easement is terminated and the property sold, the holder of the easement will receive "a proportionate share of extinguishment proceeds" to hold for charitable purposes similar to those for which the grantor gave the easement. The Internal Revenue Service has issued regulations to describe what a "proportionate share" is.[17] They are very simple: "the donor must agree that the donation of the perpetual conservation restriction gives rise to a property right, immediately vested in the donee organization, with a fair market value that is at least equal to the proportionate value that the perpetual conservation restriction at the time of the gift, bears to the value of the property as a whole at that time."

What does this sentence mean? If at the time of the gift the property is worth $3 million, and if the gift (the conservation easement) is valued at $1 million, then the proportionate value of the easement is one third of the property value at the time of the gift. If the property is later condemned and the easement extinguished, then the agreement must provide that the holder of the conservation easement will receive at least one third of the proceeds.

What could go wrong? Consider this situation. Your clients own 300 scenic acres worth $3 million and want to build a country estate for $1 million on a ten-acre portion of the property. Your clients are willing to give the county a conservation easement over 290 acres that will preserve the 290 acres as a natural area forever. A competent appraiser values the conservation easement at $2 million, and your clients make the gift. The clients point out to you that next

---

v. Commissioner, T.C. Memo. 2018-45, the Tax Court denied a developer's deduction for granting a conservation easement over 125 acres of a 1,280-acre tract that restricted its use to be a public park, as part of the developer's sale of the 125 acres to the county, when the developer had also proposed to build a planned community on the remaining 1,155 acres and to advertise the park as an amenity of the planned community.

[17] 26 CFR § 1.170A-14(g)(6)(ii).

year they will build their expensive dream home on a corner of the property. You provide in your conservation easement agreement that in the unlikely event that the easement is terminated, your clients will receive the value of their future improvements and the rest of the money (i.e., the land value) will be divided between your clients and the easement holder in today's proportions: two thirds to the county and one third to your clients. That seems very reasonable, and it is in fact reasonable: when your clients build their house, they are adding to the value of the property, and they should get that value back if the property is condemned or the easement extinguished by a sale. For example, if several years later the property is condemned while the land value is unchanged and the house is worth $1 million, under that formula your clients would receive $2 million ($1 million for the house and $1 million for their interest in the land) and the county would receive $2 million for its interest in the land.

The problem here is that the easement holder (the county) will receive only half the proceeds, not two thirds of the proceeds. The Internal Revenue Service takes the position that if you include a formula that adjusts how the proceeds are allocated to give the landowner more than the "proportionate share" on account of improvements that the landowner makes to the property after the donation, you have disqualified the gift from being deductible. In *Cottonwood Place, LLC v. Commissioner*, the Tax Court agreed with the Internal Revenue Service.[18]

This is the troublesome paragraph in the *Cottonwood Place* donation. I've italicized the fifteen words that cost the taxpayer the deduction:

> As required under Treas. Reg. § 1.170A-14(g)(6)(ii), the parties stipulate to have a current fair market value determined by multiplying the fair market value of the Property unencumbered by this Conservation Easement *(minus any increase in value after the date of this Conservation Easement attributable to improvements)* by the ratio of the value of the Conservation Easement at the time of this conveyance to the value of the Property at the time of this conveyance without deduction

[18] Cottonwood Place, LLC v. Commissioner, T.C. Memo 2020-115

> for the value of the Conservation Easement. The value of this Conservation Easement at the time of this conveyance, and the value of the Property at the time of this conveyance without deduction for the value of the Conservation Easement, shall be determined according to that certain Property Appraisal Report, on file at the office of the Grantee, prepared on behalf of Grantor to establish the value of the gift of this Conservation Easement. The values at the time of this Conservation Easement shall be those values used to calculate the deduction for federal income tax purposes pursuant to § 170(h) of the Code.

The Tax Court's opinion implies that the provision would have passed muster if it had read as follows:

> As required under Treas. Reg. § 1.170A-14(g)(6)(ii), the parties stipulate to have a current fair market value determined by multiplying the fair market value of the Property unencumbered by this Conservation Easement *(without any adjustment to value for improvements made after the date of this Conservation Easement)* by the ratio of the value of the Conservation Easement at the time of this conveyance to the value of the Property at the time of this conveyance without deduction for the value of the Conservation Easement. The value of this Conservation Easement at the time of this conveyance, and the value of the Property at the time of this conveyance without deduction for the value of the Conservation Easement, shall be determined according to that certain Property Appraisal Report, on file at the office of the Grantee, prepared on behalf of Grantor to establish the value of the gift of this Conservation Easement. The values at the time of this Conservation Easement shall be those values used to calculate the deduction for federal income tax purposes pursuant to § 170(h) of the Code.

The Tax Court's reasoning is that if the donor gives an interest to a charity that is worth two thirds of the total value of the property at the time of the gift, under the Code and regulations the charity must receive two thirds of the value of the property when the easement is extinguished; otherwise, the two thirds of the land value that the charity receives at the time of the donation is not committed to conservation purposes in perpetuity.

What if you provide that if the property is condemned, the charity will receive at least the fair market value of the conservation easement as of the date your client granted it? The Tax Court has rejected that approach as being inconsistent with § 170(f) and (h) because if the charity does not receive any of the appreciation in value between the time of the gift and the time of condemnation, its share of the property is not remaining constant but is decreasing as the property appreciates.[19]

In researching this section, I noticed that many of the challenged easement agreements used almost identical language about adjusting the allocation of termination proceeds based on the value of improvements that the landowner adds after making the gift. I surmise that the similarity is not because the same set of lawyers drafted all of the agreements but because someone—possibly even a donee charity—drafted a form that others copied, believing that adjusting the allocation of termination proceeds to account for improvements would be fair. Even as of spring 2021, forms available online don't have language that complies with the Internal Revenue Code. For example, the Florida Fish and Wildlife Conservation Commission offers a form of conservation easement that states simply:

> 16. Condemnation. If the Conservation Easement is taken, in whole or in part, by exercise of the power of eminent domain, Grantee shall be entitled to compensation in accordance with applicable law.[20]

If your client wants to claim the tax deduction, don't use this language as it doesn't guarantee that the Conservation Commission will receive at least its proportionate share of any condemnation proceeds. Without that guarantee, the Service will challenge the deduction.

---

[19] Railroad Holdings, LLC v. Commissioner, T.C. Memo 2020-22.

[20] https://myfwc.com/media/11997/gt_conservationeasementform.pdf, retrieved March 29, 2021.

Compare the Florida language to this tax clause from the Model Grant of Conservation Easement and Declaration of Covenants, published by WeConservePA:

> **1.07(e) Extinguishment.** In accordance with §1.170A-14(g)(6) of the Regulations, the undersigned Owner or Owners agree that (1) the grant of the Conservation Easement gives rise to a real estate right, immediately vested in Holder, that entitles Holder to compensation upon extinguishment of the easement; and (2) extinguishment for unexpected changes that make impossible or impractical the continued use of the Property for conservation purposes (as defined in the Regulations) of this Grant can only be accomplished by judicial proceedings. The fair market value of the right is to be determined in accordance with the Regulations; i.e., it is at least equal to the proportionate value that the Conservation Easement as of the Easement Date bears to the value of the Property as a whole as of the Easement Date (the "Proportionate Value"). If the Proportionate Value exceeds the compensation otherwise payable to Holder under this Grant or Applicable Law, Holder is entitled to payment of the Proportionate Value. Holder must use funds received on account of the Proportionate Value for conservation purposes (as defined in the Regulations).[21]

In contrast to the Florida clause, the Pennsylvania clause closely tracks the requirements of the tax code and its regulations. The definition of "Proportionate Value" is exactly as stated in the regulations, and there is no fiddling with the Proportionate Value on account of any later improvements to the property. The Pennsylvania clause also contains a requirement that the holder of the easement must use condemnation proceeds for conservation purposes.

Even if the donee organization supplies a form of conservation easement, if your client is expecting to claim a charitable deduction for the easement, you must evaluate the form yourself and confirm that it complies with the requirements of the tax code. Don't take the

---

[21] https://conservationtools-production.s3.amazonaws.com/library_item_files/323/2490/CE_model_and_commentary_201027.pdf, retrieved March 29, 2021.

word of an entity that doesn't pay federal income tax: check the form and the requirements for yourself.

3.3.1.5 The Fifth Requirement, Valuation, Is Sometimes Abused

Although it's not part of drafting the conservation easement agreement, if you are advising prospective donors of a conservation easement you should be clear with them about the appraisal requirements. If the landowner intends to claim a charitable deduction of more than $5,000 for the gift, then the landowner must obtain a qualified appraisal to support the claimed deduction, and must attach the appraisal to the landowner's tax return if the deduction is more than $500,000.[22] The Internal Revenue Service has vigorously pursued taxpayers who claim large deductions for donating conservation easements over land that the taxpayers bought for far lower prices. For example, in the *Railroad Holdings* case, the taxpayer's affiliate bought 454 acres of land for $4 million in 2008. In 2012, through various transfers among affiliates, Railroad Holdings came to own 452 of the 454 acres. In December 2012, Railroad Holdings contributed a conservation easement over the 452 acres to a qualified recipient and claimed a deduction of $16 million for the charitable contribution. The Tax Court denied the deduction that Railroad Holdings claimed on other grounds. Would the claimed value have stood up to a challenge by the Service? It seems unlikely.

If you don't regularly prepare gift tax returns, or if you are not familiar with both the state and federal requirements for claiming a charitable deduction for the gift of a conservation easement, insist that your client consult a knowledgeable accountant and obtain a proper appraisal before your client makes the gift, claims the deduction, and nervously awaits the running of the statute of limitations.

---

22 IRC § 170(f)(11).

4
General Drafting Principles for Appurtenant Easements

Easements in gross and easements appurtenant both burden specific property. The difference between easements in gross and easements appurtenant is that easements appurtenant also benefit specific property, and the right to use an easement appurtenant passes with title to the benefited property. It's therefore important when you draft an easement appurtenant to identify not just the burdened property but also the benefited property. Here are a few basic principles to keep in mind when you draft an easement appurtenant.

4.1 Identify the Burdened Property

If you have examined the title to a tract of farmland, you may have found an old easement that reads "John and Jane Smith grant an easement to Bill and Mary Jones for a thirty-foot wide driveway over the Smith tract for the benefit of the land that the grantees own that's adjacent to the grantors' land." I've occasionally encountered old easements in that form that identify the grantors' tract but not the grantees' tract, or that identify the grantees' tract but not the grantors' tract.

In 1886, everyone in the county knew where the Smiths and Joneses lived and where their farms were. Today, part of the Smith farm is about to be subdivided. Is it subject to the easement or not? The developer and the lender would like to know—and the ancient easement agreement doesn't say. Don't create this problem for future owners; identify the tract that the grantors own. I will start an easement agreement with recitals, one of which reads "Grantors own the real property described on the attached Exhibit A (the 'Grantor Tract'), incorporated herein by this reference." Exhibit A contains the legal description of the grantors' property. Even though the easement may affect only a portion of the Grantor Tract, I want to include the description of the entire tract of which the easement area is a part because I want to make it as easy as possible for future title searchers to find the easement and determine that it affects the Grantor Tract, which means using a legal description for the Grantor Tract that matches something already on the public record.

4.2 Identify the Portion of the Burdened Property That Is Actually Affected

The Smith farm (the Grantor Tract) may cover forty acres, but the Joneses don't want or need all forty acres for their driveway. If you represent the Smiths, you don't want to encumber the entire farm with the driveway easement—some day the Smiths may want to subdivide.

I routinely specify as exactly as possible which part of the Grantor Tract will be subject to the easement. I include a recital that the grantors are granting the easement over only a portion of the Grantor Tract, and in the granting clause I define and specify the easement area. For example, the recital might read:

> C. Grantee wishes to acquire an access easement over the portion of the Grantor Tract legally described on the attached Exhibit C (the "Easement Area"), incorporated herein by this reference. Grantor is willing to grant to Grantee an access easement over the Easement Area, on the terms and conditions of this Agreement.

The granting clause in the easement agreement might read as follows:

> 2. Grantor grants to Grantee, for the benefit of the Grantee Tract, a permanent non-exclusive easement for pedestrian and vehicle ingress and egress over the portion of the Grantor Tract described herein as the Easement Area.

4.3 Identify the Benefited Property

It's important to identify the burdened property and the portion of the burdened property that is subject to the easement. It's equally important to identify the benefited property, not just so that the grantor and grantee know what property the easement will benefit, but so that future owners of the properties will know who can and can't use the easement. Consider our informal easement agreement from 1886. If it didn't contain a legal description of the Jones tract then today it will take some effort to figure out which units of land have the right to use the easement area, because to answer the question we will need to research what land the Joneses owned in 1886. For that reason, I include in every easement appurtenant a recital that the grantees own the Grantee Tract and a statement in the granting clause (see the previous section) that the easement is for the benefit of the Grantee Tract. If its legal description is a simple lot and block, then I include the legal description of the Grantee Tract in the appropriate recital:

> B. Grantees own Lot 4, Block 5, ASPHALT HEIGHTS, a subdivision of record in Multnomah County, Oregon, hereinafter the "Grantee Tract."

If its legal description is longer, then I will write the recital like this instead:

> B. Grantees own a tract of land in Multnomah County, Oregon (the "Grantee Tract") located generally in Sections 24 and 25, Township 1 South, Range 1 East of the Willamette Meridian, and more specifically described on the attached Exhibit B, incorporated herein by this reference.

I'll then place the full legal description of the Grantee Tract in Exhibit B. As with my description of the Grantor Tract, I want the description of the Grantee Tract to match as much as possible a description that's already been recorded. If the grantor is giving the easement to benefit only a portion of the Grantee Tract, then I'll include separate descriptions of the Grantee Tract (the entire parcel that the grantees own) and the "Benefited Property" (the portion of the Grantee Tract that gets the benefit of the easement). Usually, however, the grantee is obtaining the easement to benefit the entire tract that the grantee owns.

4.4 Limitations on Use

Twenty-five hundred years ago the philosopher Heraclitus wrote, "Nothing is permanent except change." Keep this thought in mind when you are drafting an easement. How might the use of the burdened and benefited properties change over the years?

For example, the Grantee wants to acquire an access easement over the Grantor's acreage to get to a public road from the Grantee's house and land, as shown in Figure 4.1.

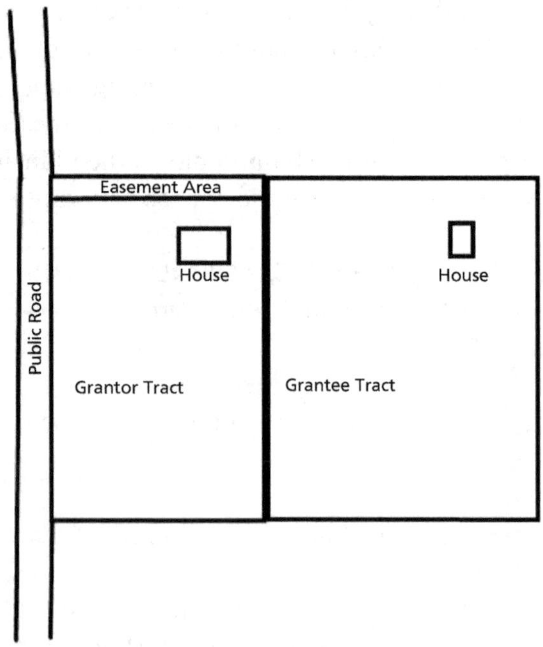

Figure 4.1 The easement to the farmhouse

For a modest sum, the Grantor may be willing to grant a permanent right to the Grantee to have a driveway pass through the Grantor Tract, or to share the use of the Grantor's driveway, and to allow the Grantee to run utility lines from the public road to the Grantee's house. The additional traffic past the Grantor's house that one additional house would create is small, and the parties are on friendly terms. The Grantor and the Grantee might describe the easement simply as being for "ingress, egress, and utilities," and allow the Grantee to pave the easement area if the Grantee wishes.

Some years later, the Grantor Tract and the Grantee Tract have passed into the hands of others. The area is no longer rural, and the farms and small lots are giving way to subdivisions. The new owner of the Grantee Tract has a plan (shown in Figure 4.2).

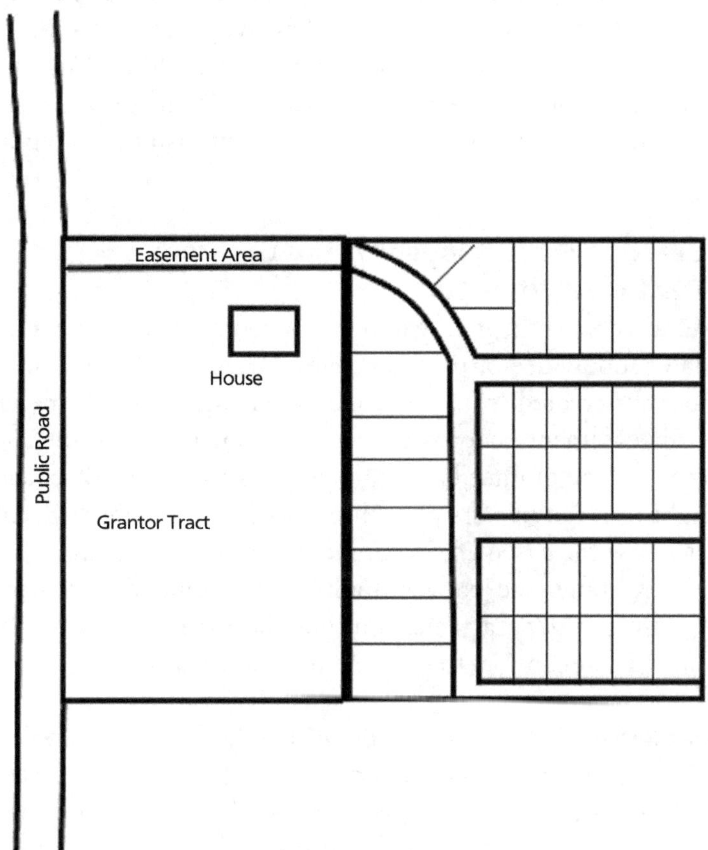

Figure 4.2 Will the easement serve the subdivision?

"One moment, please," says the owner of the Grantor Tract to the owner of the Grantee Tract. "The easement from 50 years ago was for access to one house, not to a 40-lot subdivision. You can't use your one-house easement for 40 houses."

The developer responds: "The easement says that I can use it for ingress, egress, and utilities to benefit the Grantee Tract. I want to use it for ingress, egress, and utilities to benefit the Grantee Tract. And think of the benefits! I'll widen and pave it."

How could the original grantor and grantee have avoided the later owners—possibly their children and grandchildren—getting into this nasty and expensive dispute?

A grantor of an easement should limit the physical extent of the grantee's use by describing the specific portion of the grantor's property that the grantee can use. A grantor does not say "I grant you an easement to build and use a driveway across my property," but says instead "I grant you an easement to build and use a driveway across the north 20 feet of my property." The grantor can also limit the purpose of the easement and the intensity of the grantee's use. Let's see how.

4.4.1 Describe What Happens if the Grantee Tract Is Partitioned

The general rule is that if an easement benefits an entire tract and the tract is later subdivided or partitioned, the easement benefits each of the lots or parcels created from the original benefited tract. If the grantor granted an easement to provide access to all of the grantee's tract, Blackacre, and the grantee later subdivides or partitions Blackacre into six or eight lots, the owners of each of those six or eight lots will have the right to use the easement in common with one another.

In this example, the parties might have included a provision to deviate from the general rule, limiting the easement to use by one parcel only. For example, they could have agreed:

> This easement is intended to benefit only one lot or parcel. If the Grantee Tract is subdivided or partitioned, then the Grantee shall designate one and only one of the resulting lots or parcels to continue to enjoy the benefit of the easement, and the right of the other resulting lots or parcels to enjoy the benefit of the

easement will terminate. If Grantee makes no such designation on the subdivision or partition plat, then the easement will benefit only the one lot or parcel closest to the Easement Area, and none of the others.

This is not a perfect solution. What happens if the grantee develops Blackacre with a forty-unit apartment house? Blackacre is still just one parcel, but it has forty times the inhabitants, and they will put forty times the burden on the access easement. The answer is to limit the intensity of the use.

4.4.2 Limit the Intensity of Use of the Easement Area

Another way for the grantor to prevent the one-house driveway from becoming the service route to a subdivision or the main entrance to an apartment complex is to limit the intensity of use of the easement area. The grantee of long ago might have contemplated building a second or even a third house on the farm and might have bargained for that right. Conversely, the grantor might have been willing to allow the use of the driveway for one, two, or three houses, but not for forty. They could have included this provision in the easement agreement:

> The scope and use of the easement area are limited to ingress, egress, and utility service to [one single-family residence] [two / three single-family residences] and [its / their] appurtenant outbuildings.

The grantee can still build one or two more houses on Blackacre whose occupants will use the easement. If the grantee builds a large apartment on Blackacre, the grantee will have to go back to the grantor and ask to buy a more expansive (and expensive) easement or will have to find access to the apartment across some other property.

4.4.3 Limit the Land Uses That the Easement Area Can Serve

The careful drafter can limit the intensity of the grantee's use of the easement by quantity, such as in the previous example limiting the grantee to using the easement for one, two, or three houses. A careful drafter can also protect the grantor by limiting the land uses that the easement area can serve. Let's expand on the language from section 4.4.2 by limiting not only the number of houses that can use the easement area, but also by prohibiting the grantee from using the easement to benefit any nonresidential purpose on the grantee's tract:

> The scope and use of the easement area are limited to ingress, egress, and utility service to [one single-family residence] [two / three single-family residences] and [its / their] appurtenant outbuildings. Under no circumstances may the Grantee use the Easement Area for access to more than [one single-family residence] [two / three single family residences] and their appurtenant outbuildings, nor for any multi-family, commercial, institutional, industrial, or other non-residential purpose.[1]

4.4.4 Limit the Dimensions and Capacity of Roads and Utilities

The grantor can also limit the grantee's use of the easement area and guard against the easement becoming overburdened by imposing other quantitative restrictions on the easement. For access easements, the width of the easement area limits the width of a road. If the easement area is only twenty feet wide, the grantee can't build a forty-foot-wide road because the road won't fit into the easement area.

If the easement area will hold both a road and utilities, then the grantor should limit the width of the road to be somewhat less than the width of the easement area so that room is left for the utilities. For example, if the easement area is thirty feet wide then the parties can limit the road to twenty feet, leaving a ten-foot strip alongside the road (or possibly five feet on each side of the road) for overhead and underground utilities:

> Grantee may construct a private access road up to [20] feet wide within the Easement Area to serve the house on the Grantee Tract. Grantee may use the rest of the Easement Area

---

[1] I eschew redundancy in drafting, but if a business point is important to your client, then it's worth repeating, which is why I suggest writing not only what is allowed, but what is prohibited.

for overhead power, cable television, and telephone lines and underground water, sewer, and natural gas lines[2] to serve the house on the Grantee Tract.

If the grantee plans to build several houses on the grantee's property, or if the grantor plans to use part of the private road in common with the grantee, then both parties should consult the local zoning code's requirements for the minimum width of private driveways. I have seen local codes that say that a private driveway that serves two houses must be *X* feet wide, one that serves three or four houses must be *Y* feet wide, and one that serves more than four houses must be *Z* feet wide. If you represent a grantee who wants to use the accessway to serve four houses and you negotiate an easement that isn't wide enough to hold both the minimum required road to serve the four houses and have room on the side for utility lines, your client will be unhappy with you when the building department denies the permit for the third house because the accessway is not wide enough to comply with code.

A grantor who is your client may not mind that the easement area is too narrow for the *grantee* to build a third or fourth house. The grantor may, however, complain if the *grantor* wants to attach another house to the common driveway and is turned down by the building department for the same reason. The grantor will then have the unwelcome choice between widening the driveway (potentially opening up the grantee's land for increased development that the grantor does not want) or abandoning the grantor's own development plans.

In response to the previous paragraph, the attentive reader will observe that if the easement covers an access road that is twenty feet wide, the grantor can widen the road by four feet on the grantor's property, outside of the easement area, without giving the grantee any right to use the additional four feet of roadway for access to the grantee's property. That is the correct law school answer: the grantee's rights extend only to what was granted.

---

2 Omit or forbid any specific utility services that the grantor does *not* want within the Easement Area. The grantor may object to having a natural gas line in the Easement Area, and in a rural area gas service may not even be available.

4.4.5 Pass-Through Rights

As I noted in section 4.3, an easement appurtenant to a particular property benefits only that property. A common source of litigation about easements is when the owner of a benefited property ("Tract Two") who has an easement to cross a burdened property ("Tract One") grants an easement across Tract Two for the benefit of a third property ("Tract Three") who intends to use the Tract Two easement to reach and cross the Tract One easement. An example is shown in Figure 4.3.

Once upon a time, the owner of Tract One gave the owner of Tract Two an access easement over "Easement 1" for the benefit of Tract Two. The owner of Tract Three now wants to get to the public road and offers to buy an access easement across "Easement 2" from the owner of Tract Two, which will let the Tract Three owner get to Easement 1. Will the Tract Three owner then be able to cross over Easement 1 to get to the public road, even though Tract One granted the right to use Easement 1 only to Tract Two? Or may the owner of Tract One sue the owner of Tract Three for trespass if Tract Three tries to cross Tract One?

The question of pass-through rights is something like cabotage in international shipping and airline travel: may a shipping line or airline from Nation One that has the right to carry passengers or freight from Nation One to two different cities in Nation Two also carry passengers or freight between those two cities in Nation Two?

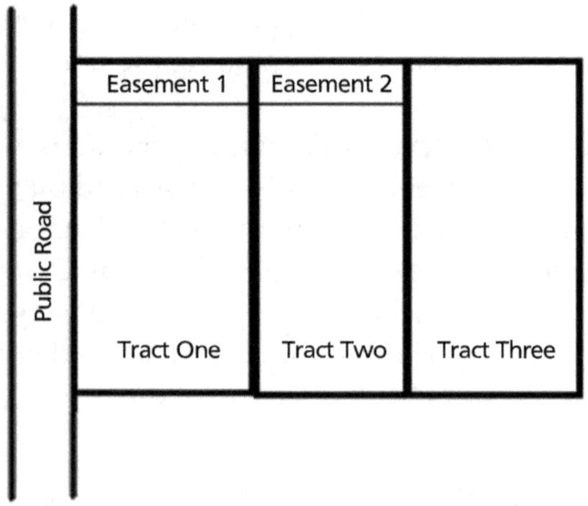

Figure 4.3 Cabotage, or pass-through rights, illustrated

In the case of easements, the question whether Tract Two can give Tract Three pass-through rights over Easement 1 is the contention in many reported cases,[3] going back to at least 1839.[4] Usually the owner of Tract Three loses.

The general principle is that the owner of an easement appurtenant to his or her property (the Tract Twos of the world) across a burdened property (the Tract Ones) cannot share the benefit of the easement with property to which the easement is not already appurtenant (the Tract Threes). Put in simpler terms, if the easement is limited to benefit Tract Two only, the owner of Tract Two can't expand its use beyond Tract Two.

Although the general principle is well established, if you represent the grantor then you can include a clause in the easement agreement to make the point clear. You can even impose an affirmative duty on the grantee to protect your right to exclude the Tract Threes of the world from using your land. Here is one way to say so:

> Grantor is granting the rights described in this Agreement solely for the benefit of the Grantee Tract, and for no other property.

---

3 For example, in College Inns of America, Inc. v. Cully, 254 Or 375 (1969), a grantor created a private road, Ferry Lane, and gave the owners of all adjoining tracts the right to use the road for vehicular and pedestrian traffic. The plaintiff acquired a tract that bordered Ferry Lane, and an adjoining tract that did not border Ferry Lane. The plaintiff built a large college dormitory on its combined tract and used Ferry Lane for access to the dormitory. Only a small part of the dormitory was on the original Ferry Lane tract. One of the other Ferry Lane owners blocked the plaintiff's use of Ferry Lane on the ground that the plaintiff was using Ferry Lane not just to benefit the original tract that adjoined Ferry Lane but also for access to the part of the dormitory that was not covered by the easement. The plaintiff sued for an injunction to stop the defendant from interfering with its use of Ferry Lane for access to the dormitory and lost at trial and on appeal. *See also, e.g.*, Beloit Foundry Co. v. Ryan, 28 Ill. 2d. 379 (1963); Murphy v. Mart Realty of Brockton, Inc., 348 Mass. 675 (1965) ("A right of way appurtenant to the land conveyed cannot be used by the owner of the dominant tenement to pass to or from other land adjacent to or beyond that to which the easement is appurtenant"), and McCullough v. Broad Exchange Co., 101 App. Div. 566 (N.Y. 1905), *affirmed* 184 N.Y. 592 (1906), holding that an easement holder forfeited its access easement through overuse when it combined the benefited tract with a tract that did not enjoy the easement, built an office building on the combined tract, and used the easement for access to the building.

4 Davenport v. Lamson, 21 Pick. 72 (Mass. 1839), cited in Stearns v. Mullen, 70 Mass. 151 (1855).

Grantee covenants to Grantor that Grantee will not permit any person claiming by, through, or under Grantee to use the Easement Area for access to or from any property other than the Grantee Tract.

If you represent a grantee who contemplates acquiring other property in the area and who will want to use the easement area for access to that other property, then you must declare that right in the easement agreement. Your client owns Tract A shown on the map in Figure 4.4. Your client would like to acquire Tract B and Tract C in the future and use an accessway (not shown) across the Grantor Tract for services to the combined development. Your client doesn't want to buy any access right or provide any benefit to the owners of Tract B and Tract C now, but wants to be able to use the easement across the Grantor Tract to get to Tract B and Tract C if your client buys them in the future.

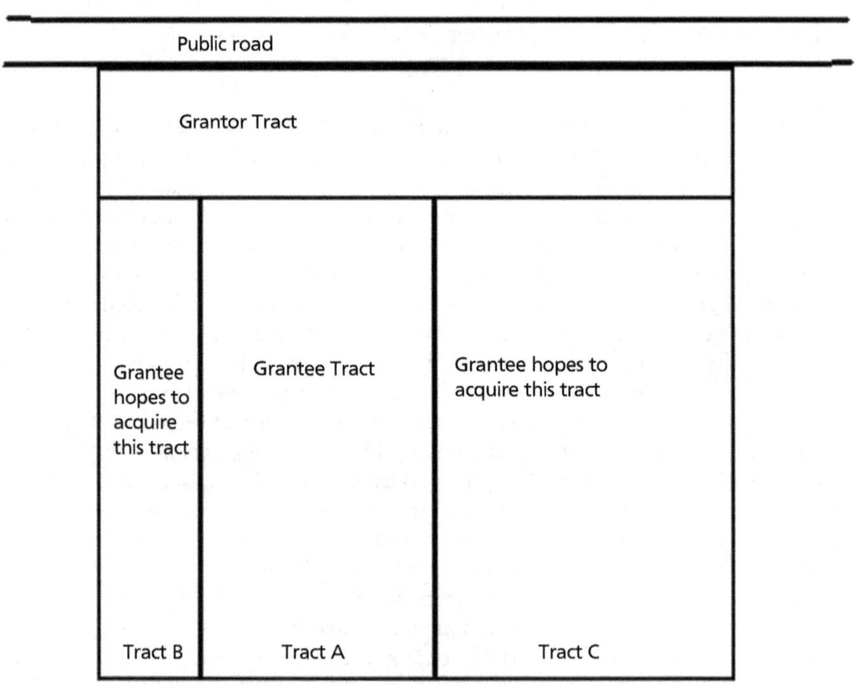

Figure 4.4 Benefiting land that the grantee doesn't own yet

Here is one way to write the granting clause that will extend the benefit of the easement to the land that the grantee hopes or expects to acquire, but doesn't yet own:

> Grantor is granting the rights described in this Agreement solely to benefit the Grantee Tract at present. Grantor and Grantee contemplate that in the future one or both of the tracts depicted on the attached Exhibit ___ as "Tract B" and "Tract C" may come under common ownership with the Grantee Tract, and in that event the right to use the Easement Area and the other benefits of this Agreement will extend to the tract or tracts that come under common ownership with the Grantee Tract. [Optional addition: The rights described in this Agreement will continue to benefit the tracts that come under common ownership with the Grantee Tract notwithstanding that they may later be subdivided, partitioned, or separately owned.]

4.5 Repairs and Maintenance

A good easement agreement will specify (a) at what level the users will maintain the easement area, (b) how they will allocate the cost to maintain and repair the easement area, and (c) how they will collect the funds to pay the cost. If only one party is using the easement, that party should pay all of the cost to maintain the facilities in the easement area. If several parties are sharing the use of the easement area, their agreement should allocate the cost and provide a mechanism to pay that cost.

Most commonly, the shared costs are to maintain and repair a shared driveway or access road. Your easement agreement should state how the parties will allocate the cost to maintain the easement. If you do not specify how to allocate the costs, your state may do it for you. For instance, Oregon provides the following default language at ORS 105.175(3):

> (3) The cost of maintaining the easement in repair in the absence of an agreement and in the absence of maintenance provisions in a recorded instrument creating the easement shall be shared

> by each holder of an interest in the easement in proportion to the use made of the easement by each holder of an interest in the easement.

California provides a similar default allocation at Cal. Civ. Code § 845(c):

> (c) In the absence of an agreement, the cost shall be shared proportionately to the use made of the easement by each owner.

As of this writing (spring 2021), Illinois, Texas, Florida, and many other states have not adopted similar statutes to allocate the costs to maintain an easement. Massachusetts recognizes a common-law right of contribution among easement holders to maintain the easement.[5]

You should not leave it up to an unknown judge's future interpretation of your state's common law to determine how to allocate maintenance costs. If your clients are content to allocate the costs in accordance with your state's statutory default provisions, why not say so in your agreement? You could write:

> The parties will allocate the costs to maintain and repair the roadway in the Easement Area in accordance with [ORS 105.175] [Cal. Civ. Code §845] [the applicable provision in your state].

Be aware, however, that if the legislature changes the statute, the legislature is in effect amending your agreement. If you like your state's current statutory provisions, instead of incorporating them by reference, you could copy them word for word and put the current provisions into your agreement. You've then reserved for the parties the power to change the allocation in the future.

Assuming that you're not going to rely on your state's statutory or common-law method to allocate costs, let's look at how you can

---

[5] Shapiro v. Burton, 23 Mass. App. Ct. 327, 335 (1987), remanding to the trial court the question of determining "how the costs should be equitably apportioned among the common easement owners" to maintain a stairway from their properties to the adjoining beach.

draft a clause to cover maintenance and repairs, moving from the general to the specific. You can be very general:

> The parties will share equally in the cost to maintain the road surface in good condition.

This simple sentence covers how to allocate maintenance costs, but it leaves a hole because it doesn't define "good condition." What do the parties mean by "good condition"? The owner of an all-wheel-drive pickup truck may read "good condition" differently from the owner of a Ferrari. You can be more specific about the level to which the road will be improved, and you can define what the parties will accept as being "good condition":

> The parties will share equally in the cost to maintain the road surface as a 12-foot-wide graveled strip, suitable for travel in all seasons and bladed (smoothed or graded) once a year. A party who wishes to improve the road surface above this standard may do so, at that party's sole expense.

We've now set a standard beyond which one user can't force the others to share in the cost to upgrade the road. The Ferrari owner can't force the pickup owner to share in the cost to pave the access road for the convenience of the Ferrari owner.

The next step is to state who will contract and pay for the maintenance. The simplest case is a driveway that is used only by the benefited tract and not at all by the burdened tract: a private driveway that happens to cross someone else's property.

> Grantee will arrange for and pay the cost to maintain the roadway in the Easement Area.

If both the Grantor and the Grantee use the driveway (as for instance if the Grantee's driveway is an extension of the Grantor's existing driveway), then you can be almost as concise:

> Grantor will arrange for and pay the cost to maintain the roadway in the Easement Area. Grantee will reimburse Grantor for

[one-half] [an equal share] [___%] of Grantor's cost within 30 days after Grantor notifies Grantee that Grantor has incurred expenses to maintain the roadway.

4.6 Change of Grade

It is a principle of easement law that the grantee of an easement has the right to make reasonable improvements in the easement area that the law requires, that are consistent with the easement agreement, and that are necessary or appropriate to the easement holder's allowed use. For example, unless the easement agreement prohibits it, the holder of an access easement can pave or gravel the accessway, smooth the road surface, fill potholes, and the like, all for the purpose of making the road safer and easier for the easement holder to use.

Does an easement holder's right to modify the easement area for its intended purpose extend to changing the grade of the easement area? Unless the easement area runs through flat land, consider including a restriction on changing the road grade in your easement agreement.

What can go wrong if the easement agreement doesn't discuss the road grade? One example is the case of *Hood v. Neil*, 502 So. 2nd 749 (Ala. 1987).

The Hoods and Neil owned adjoining land on the downhill side of Murray Hill Road near Birmingham, Alabama. Neil's property was a large homesite; the Hoods owned five acres, and Hood had used an accessway that crossed over a corner of Neil's property since 1948. Part of the accessway also served Neil's lot. Neil built a new house in 1980 and discovered that to use his driveway he would have to lower the grade of the easement area by five feet, which would have cut off the Hoods' driveway. He asked the Hoods for permission to regrade their driveway (the portion on the Hoods' property) to meet the new grade of the easement. They refused. Neil regraded his driveway and the Hoods sued. At trial, the Hoods were awarded damages for the interference with their easement. The court did not, however, grant their request for an injunction to make Neil restore the driveway to its former grade.[6]

---

[6] The current owner of the Hood tract (January 2021) told the author that he and his wife bought the Hood tract some years after the litigation and built a house

How might you avoid your client encountering the same problem that the Hoods faced when Neil dropped the driveway five feet? You could include a clause like this one:

> Grantor and Grantee intend to share the use of the Easement Area for common access to the Grantor Tract and the Grantee Tract; therefore, neither Grantor nor Grantee may change the grade or elevation of the driveway in the Easement Area without the prior written consent of the other.

If you want to give more control to the grantee, or if the driveway in the Easement Area will be for the sole benefit of the grantee, then you could use the following clause instead:

> The driveway that Grantee will build in the Easement Area is for the primary use and convenience of Grantee and the enjoyment of the Grantee Tract. Grantee will construct the driveway at a grade and slope that is suitable for Grantee's use. Grantor will not change or alter the grade and slope of the driveway without the prior written consent of Grantee.

4.7 Illustrating the Easement: A Word Is Worth Only One Thousandth of a Picture

I like maps. I especially like maps as exhibits to easement agreements. A map makes clear what words may obscure. Even in the simplest of easement agreements, I encourage my clients to include a map or sketch of the easement area that shows its relation to the grantor tract, the grantee tract, and any improvements that are relevant to the easement.

In the good old days, Farmer Smith might have conveyed a tract to Farmer Jones "together with the right to use the existing private road over the lands retained by Farmer Smith." Smith and Jones knew where the road was, but their successors 100 years later

---

with a driveway that runs to the downhill street. They don't use the Hood driveway at all, and in fact didn't know that the Hoods had had a driveway that ran through the Neil property to Murray Hill Avenue.

(i.e., you and I) don't.[7] Even if Farmers Smith and Jones weren't going to be persuaded by any lawyer in 1920 to hire a surveyor to prepare a proper legal description, they would have saved their descendants, title companies, and lenders' counsel many headaches had they included a sketch of where the road was in relation to the Smith tract and the Jones tract.

A map is especially useful (by which I mean "essential") if the easement's purpose is to allow the grantee to build underground improvements, or to validate the grantee's right to maintain underground improvements that the grantee has already built and that are not obvious on the surface, such as underground power and telephone lines, natural gas supply lines, and septic drainfields. A buyer of a property can identify the driveway and try to work out whether it's the one covered by the ancient Smith-Jones easement. But how will the buyer identify the area not to plow or pave because it's the neighbor's drainfield? A map succeeds where words merely suggest.

A good map or sketch will have not only the location and dimensions of the easement area but also some suggestion of where the easement area is in relation to nearby roads and improvements, if there are any. Even surveys for purposes other than easements should include some useful information about what is actually on the ground. The survey in Figure 4.5 is intended to show how the surveyor has marked the corners of a tract created from portions of Lots 1 and 2 of a subdivision platted a few years earlier, as well as the dimensions, shape, and location of the tract in relation to nearby streets.

Compare Figure 4.5 with a less informative survey of land less than two miles away (Figure 4.6), which is also intended to show how the surveyor marked the boundaries of a smaller tract carved from a larger tract.

The first survey does not identify buildings, but it does identify the adjoining streets and the distance from the nearest intersection. If your client were about to buy the tract that the first survey depicts you could tell your client how to search for the monuments that mark the lot corners. Not so if your client were intending to buy the tract set off in the second survey.

---

7 See section 4.1.

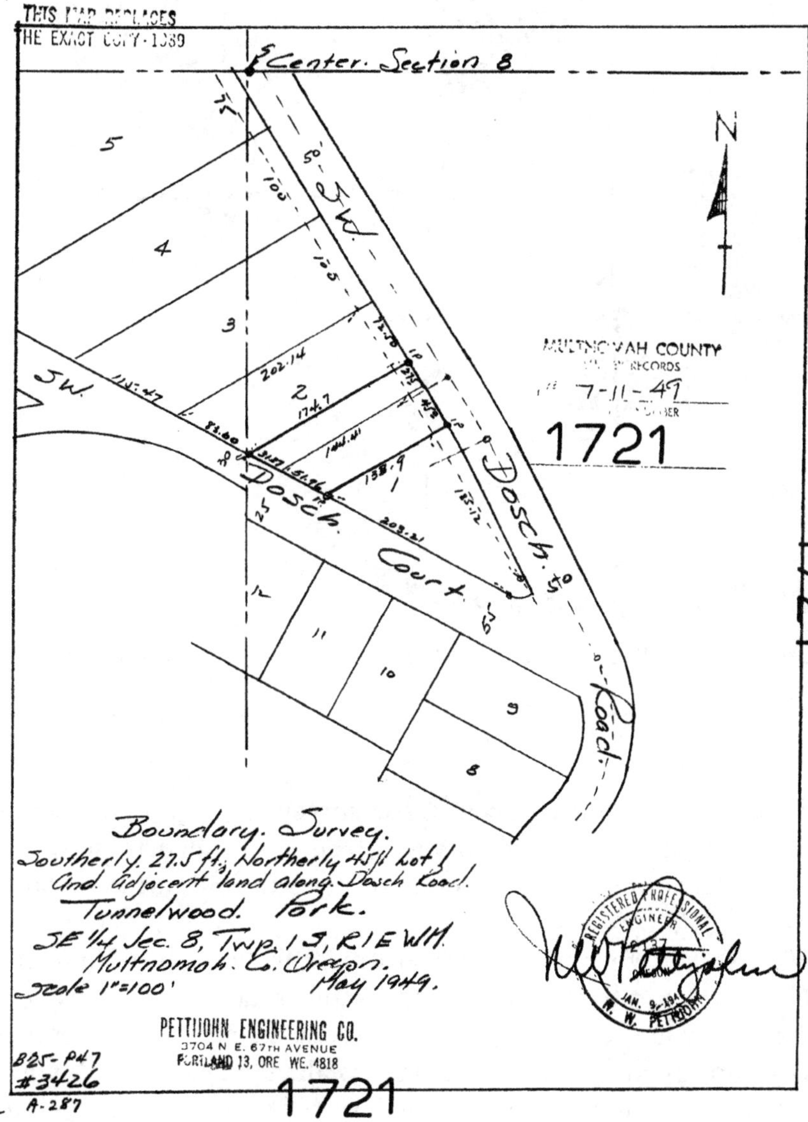

Figure 4.5 A survey to show how the corners of a new tract were marked

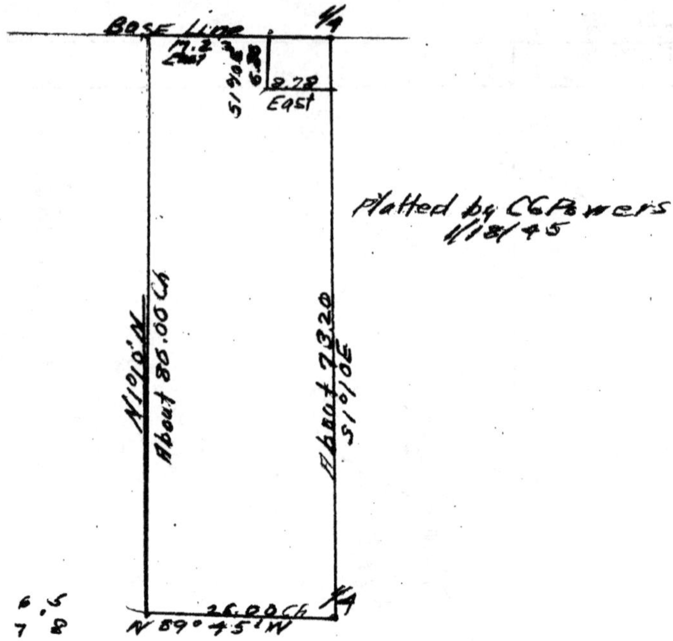

Figure 4.6 Another survey to show how the corners of a new tract were marked

Compare the information in those surveys to Figure 4.7, which shows a portion of a third survey, which is intended to show the location of a house in relation to the west, north, and east boundaries of its lot.

What should your map of the easement include? If you imagine Figure 4.1 as the base form and then add distances and directions to the map, you should be close. If I were using Figure 4.1 as a base map for an easement for a road that has already been built, I would ask the surveyor to indicate the boundaries of the road as built within the easement area (the edges of the pavement or gravel) to show the road's approximate relation to the easement area.

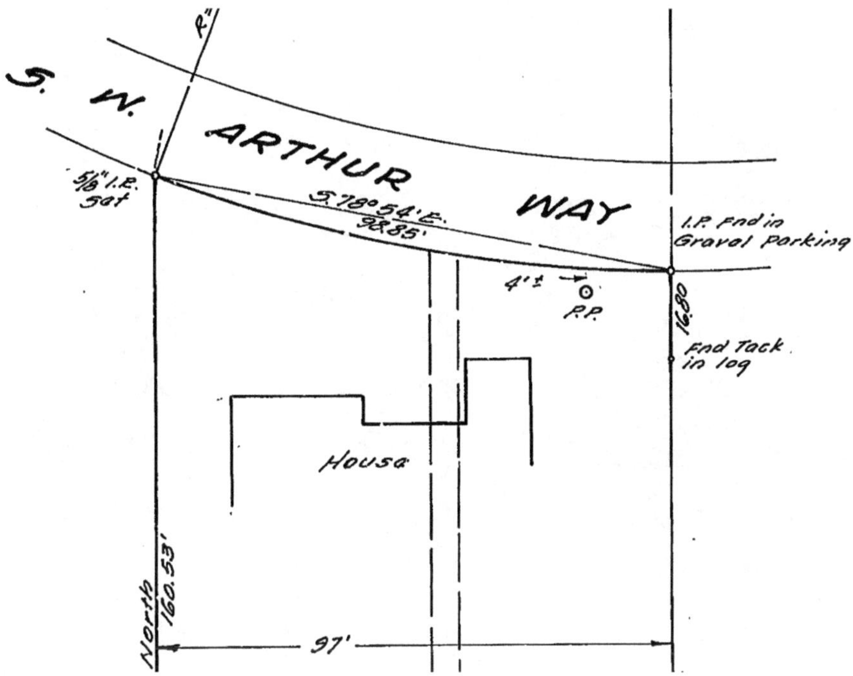

Figure 4.7 A survey with boundary lines, boundary markers, and improvements[8]

[8] Note to the curious: the dashed lines that run through the house do not indicate an easement through the dining room and kitchen. They're the boundaries of a public alley that was vacated some years before the house was built.

5
Driveway and Access Easements

I am hired to write more access easement agreements than any other class of easement. Access easements are the classic easement: a right to use one property that is appurtenant to another property. They are simple to draft, simple to document, and simple to mess up. They burden one property and benefit another property. How hard can it be to write an access easement properly? After all, it's just a driveway.

Let's begin. Chapter 4 covered some of these principles in general terms. Here I will discuss how those principles and others apply specifically to driveway and access easements.

5.1 Where Is the Easement?

As with any other easement, start by identifying the easement area.[1] What portion of the burdened property (let's call it Blackacre, or the "Grantor Tract" in the easement agreement) can be used by the owner of the benefited property (let's call it Whiteacre, or the "Grantee Tract" in the easement agreement)?

[1] See also the general discussion in section 4.2 on identifying the easement area.

If the easement area is less than all of Blackacre, then don't identify all of Blackacre as being subject to the easement. *Don't* write the granting clause like this one:

> 2. Grantor grants Grantee a permanent, nonexclusive easement for access across the Grantor Tract for the benefit of the Grantee Tract.

Why not? A title insurance company that reads this granting clause will not be able to determine where the easement area actually is, and a lender on new construction won't be able to tell whether the building it intends to finance is sitting in the easement area, which makes the Grantor Tract, practically speaking, unbuildable.

Here's a slight improvement on the granting clause—but don't use this granting clause either.

> 2. Grantor grants Grantee a permanent, nonexclusive easement for access to the Grantee Tract over and across a 20-foot-wide strip of the Grantor Tract.

At least this granting clause makes it clear that the grantee's easement does not encumber all of Blackacre, but only a twenty-foot-wide strip of Blackacre. But where is the twenty-foot-wide easement area? As with the first clause, the title insurance company cannot determine where the easement area is, which means that it's going to be difficult to find financing for a new building on Blackacre, unless the owner of Blackacre can persuade the neighbor to amend the agreement to specify which twenty feet of Blackacre the owner of Whiteacre may use. In a pinch the owner of Blackacre may sue the owner of Whiteacre and seek a declaratory judgment stating where the easement area is located. That's an expensive way to solve a drafting problem.

If Blackacre is rectangular and oriented mostly in line with compass points, and if the easement area is to run along one edge of Blackacre, then you may be able to describe the easement area as simply as this:

> 2. Grantor grants Grantee a permanent, non-exclusive easement for access to and from the Grantee Tract across the north 20.00 feet of the Grantor Tract, measured perpendicularly to

the northerly property line of the Grantor Tract, on the terms and conditions of this Agreement. This 20-foot-wide strip of the Grantor Tract is the "Easement Area."

If the easement area can't be described so simply, then attach a map that shows Blackacre, Whiteacre, and the easement area, and write the granting clause like this:

2. Grantor grants Grantee a permanent, non-exclusive easement for access to and from the Grantee Tract across a portion of the Grantor Tract 20.00 feet wide (the "Easement Area"), depicted on the attached Exhibit C[2] and legally described on the attached Exhibit D, incorporated into this Agreement by this reference.

The reader will understand from this clause that the easement burdens only a portion of Blackacre, and will be able to work out which portion is subject to the easement.

5.2 What Property Does It Benefit?

If the grantor does not want the private driveway through Blackacre to become a throughway then the easement agreement must identify what property benefits from the easement[3]—to what property is this easement appurtenant? In our example, we define Whiteacre to be the Grantee Tract and attach the legal description of Whiteacre as an exhibit to the easement agreement. Later in the easement agreement, we will restate that the easement is only for the benefit of Whiteacre:

7. This easement is an easement appurtenant to and for the benefit of the Grantee Tract only and is not an easement in gross.

[2] I usually use Exhibits A and B for the legal descriptions of the Grantor Tract and the Grantee Tract.

[3] See also the general discussion in section 4.3 on identifying the benefited property in any easement appurtenant.

5.3 How May the Grantee Use the Easement Area?

5.3.1 A Driveway Is Not Only a Driveway

The grantee's most visible use of the access easement area is going to be as a driveway.[4] If you represent the grantee, ask if the grantee will need to run utility lines to Whiteacre through Blackacre. If your client needs the easement not just for vehicle access but also for utility lines, then ask about the utilities. Sewer, water, and natural gas lines are always underground. Power, telephone, and cable may be underground or on poles, depending on the area and the utility. If you successfully negotiate a driveway easement for the owner of Whiteacre without including the right to install necessary utility lines, your client will be unhappy with you.

If you do negotiate and draft the easement to include utility lines, then give some thought to how much of the easement area will be for the driveway and how much for the utilities, particularly if wires will come in on overhead lines, because the power poles will take up some of the easement area. In section 4.4.4 I suggested this clause for an easement that would have a driveway narrower than the easement area, leaving room for overhead and underground utility lines:

> Grantee may construct a private access road up to [20] feet wide within the Easement Area to serve the house on the Grantee Tract. Grantee may use the rest of the Easement Area for overhead power, cable television, and telephone lines and underground water, sewer, and natural gas lines[5] to serve the house on the Grantee Tract.

This clause satisfies a typical grantor concern, which is that the grantee does not over-improve the easement or try to expand the easement beyond the easement area by filling up the easement area with the driveway and then claiming that the easement must be wider

---

[4] See also the general discussion in section 4.4 on limiting the grantee's use of the easement area.

[5] Omit or forbid any specific utility services that the grantor does *not* want within the easement area. The grantor may object to having a natural gas line in the easement area.

than agreed because the utility lines can't be above or beneath the driveway.

The grantee should also have a concern. It's a principle of easement law that the grantor may make any use of the easement area that does not unreasonably interfere with the grantee's use of the easement area. As long as the Blackacre owner does not unreasonably hinder Whiteacre's use of the easement, the Blackacre owner may use the easement area however the owner wishes. If the Whiteacre owner will install utility lines through the easement area, then the Whiteacre owner will want the Blackacre owner to promise not to construct improvements or plant landscaping that will block access to the utility lines if they need to be repaired. The local cable company might not mind digging up and replanting a few rose bushes to repair a break, but isn't going to remove a fifteen-foot-tall tree to do the repair.

If the grantee plans to build several houses on Whiteacre, or if the grantor plans to use part of the private road in common with the grantee, then consult the zoning code for the minimum width of private driveways. Some codes say that a private driveway that serves two houses must be *X* feet wide, one that serves three or four houses must be *Y* feet wide, and one that serves more than four houses must be *Z* feet wide. If you represent a grantee who wants to use the accessway to serve four houses on Whiteacre and you negotiate an easement that isn't wide enough to hold both the minimum required road to serve the four houses and have room on the side for utility lines, your client will be unhappy with you when the building department denies the permit for the third house on Whiteacre because the accessway is not wide enough to comply with code.

5.3.2 How Intense May the Use Be?

If you are drafting the easement agreement for the owner of Whiteacre (the grantee), then you will want the easement agreement to allow not only the use that the Whiteacre owner wants to make of the easement area now, but also some reasonable expansion of the use to accommodate what the Whiteacre owner might do later on. For example, if the easement agreement allows the grantee to use the driveway for access to one single-family dwelling, can the grantee build an accessory dwelling unit (an ADU to planners, often informally sometimes called a "mother-in-law apartment" or a "granny flat") inside or next to the house and then use the driveway for access to the ADU? If the easement agreement limits the grantee's use to one single-family dwelling, then the grantor may argue that the ADU is something beyond one single-family dwelling, particularly if the grantee is building a new structure to be the ADU instead of including it inside the existing house.

5.4 Specify Standards for the Driveway

The general legal principle is that the holder of an easement has the right to make reasonable improvements to the easement area in order to enjoy the benefit of the easement. What improvements are "reasonable"? You can let a court decide, or you can provide the standards in your easement agreement.

What improvements are reasonable depends on your point of view. In our example of Whiteacre holding an access easement through Blackacre, the owner of Blackacre may think that all the Whiteacre owner needs to build through Blackacre is a quiet dirt lane. The Whiteacre owner may want something more like the New York State Thruway. Between those two extremes lies what is reasonable.

The two basics to specify in the easement agreement are the roadway width and the roadway surface. You can specify them together in a single clause. If the driveway will serve only Whiteacre (meaning that Blackacre has its own driveway, not in the easement area), then the Blackacre owner will want to limit how wide the Whiteacre owner can build the driveway. The Blackacre owner may be less concerned with the surface. Drivers drive more slowly on gravel than on a paved driveway, but they make more noise and kick up dust than drivers on a smooth paved road.

Here are two sample clauses that specify a road surface and maximum width:

> IV. Grantee may improve the Easement Area with one driveway of up to ____ feet in width. Grantee will surface the driveway in asphalt, blacktop, or concrete [and at least annually will seal cracks and fill potholes].

Or:

> IV. Grantee may improve the Easement Area with one driveway of up to ___ feet in width, as either an all-weather gravel driveway or as a driveway paved with asphalt, blacktop, or concrete.

5.5 Gates

If several owners will share the driveway, there may come a time when one of the owners wants to install a gate across the driveway. No one should object to another user installing a gate that secures only that user's driveway if the gate does not block the other users from using the driveway. If one owner wants to install a gate where the common driveway meets the street, another owner may object to the inconvenience of having to get out of the car to open the gate, then get back in the car to drive through the gate, then get back out of the car again to close the gate.

Ask your client if the parties intend to put a gate across the shared driveway, and then either allow or prohibit it. If everyone is willing to share the cost of installing a gate, then you can include this clause:

> 7. The Owners[6] may install a [remote-controlled] gate across the Easement Area near where it joins Wind Hill Road. The Owners will set the gate far enough back from the edge of the road to allow a car to drive entirely off of Wind Hill Road and onto the driveway before opening the gate. Each Owner will pay an equal share of the cost to install, maintain, repair, and replace the gate.

Conversely, if the owners do not want any owner to install a gate, use this clause instead:

> 7. Any Owner may install a gate across the part of the driveway in the Easement Area that serves only that Owner's lot or parcel. No Owner will install any gate across any part of the driveway

---

[6] In a multiparty easement agreement, you will have defined "Owners" or "Parties" to mean and include all of the persons who are signing the agreement.

that serves more than one Owner without the written consent of all Owners whose lots or parcels are served by that part of the driveway.

5.6 Access for Everyone: Special Issues in the Multiparty Agreement

Not all access easements are as simple as Blackacre allowing Whiteacre to build and use a driveway through a part of Blackacre, with one dominant estate and one servient estate. It's common for three, four, or more users to share a driveway that runs through several properties, sometimes under a recorded easement agreement, sometimes under a series of granted or reserved easements in old deeds, and sometimes "because the road has always been there."

Here is how to proceed if a landowner hires you to prepare an easement agreement for a multi-user road. In this example, I will assume that there are five parcels in a row, named Alfa, Bravo, Charlie, Delta, and Echo, with the Alfa Tract bordering the east side of a public road and the Bravo, Charlie, Delta, and Echo Tracts laid out east of the Alfa Tract in that order, so that to get to the Echo Tract you must pass through the Alfa, Bravo, Charlie, and Delta Tracts in that order. To get to the Charlie Tract, you must pass through the Alfa and Bravo Tracts but don't need to cross the Delta and Echo Tracts. Figure 5.1 is an illustration of the five tracts that use the driveway, which is located in the Easement Area. The Easement Area is not

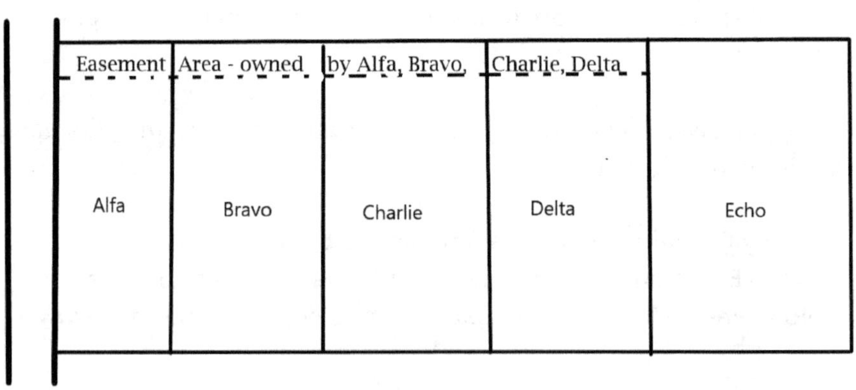

Figure 5.1 A multi-user driveway

common property; Alfa, Bravo, Charlie, and Delta each own a portion. Echo uses the entire Easement Area but does not own any of it.

5.6.1 Allocating Maintenance Cost

Consider the example in Figure 5.1. The five landowners want to sign the easement agreement that you've drafted on behalf of Alfa but one point remains to be decided: how will the five landowners allocate the maintenance costs?[7]

Your state may have a statute that allocates the cost to maintain an access easement if the parties don't agree on some other method. Oregon requires the holders of an interest in an access easement to maintain it in repair (not defined), either in accordance with an agreement or recorded document creating the easement, or if no agreement exists, "in proportion to the use made of the easement by each holder of an interest in the easement."[8]

California has a similar statute. If the owners of the easement or of the land subject to the easement have not agreed on how to share the cost to maintain the easement, then "the cost shall be shared proportionately to the use made of the easement by each owner."[9]

Not every state has such a statute. Illinois, home of the very specific Entry on Adjacent Land To Accomplish Repairs Act,[10] has no general statute allocating the cost to repair an access easement. Arizona has no general statute allocating the cost to repair, but in a case between two users of an easement has applied the doctrine of equitable contribution

---

[7] Why do you represent only Alfa and not all five landowners? Rule 1.7 of the ABA's Model Rules of Professional Conduct, adopted in some form by most (maybe all) state bars, states that, with one exception, "a lawyer shall not represent a client if the representation involves a concurrent conflict of interest," which exists if "the representation of one client will be directly adverse to another client." You can represent all five landowners if you reasonably believe that you "will be able to provide competent and diligent representation to each affected client," the representation is not prohibited by law, the representation does not involve conflicting claims in the same litigation or administrative proceeding, and each client gives informed consent in writing. The landowners may not be fighting about roadway width or surfacing—perhaps they all like blacktop—but if you explain the options for allocating maintenance costs they will disagree on which one to choose. Be safe—don't try to represent everyone.

[8] ORS 105.175, as in force in March 2021.

[9] Cal. Civ. Code § 845, as in force in March 2021.

[10] 765 ILCS §125, discussed in section 9.2 of this book.

to require the users of an access easement to contribute to maintaining and repairing the road. In allocating the costs among the easement users, the court will take into account:

> various relevant factors, which may include but are not limited to each party's proportionate use of the easement, including the amount and intensity of actual use, and the benefits derived therefrom; whether each party received proper notice and reasonable opportunity to participate in the decisions regarding repairs and maintenance; whether the completed work was reasonable and necessary; whether the repairs and maintenance were performed adequately, properly, and at a reasonable price; the value of any other contributions (monetary or in kind) by the parties to repairs and maintenance; and any other factors that may be deemed relevant.[11]

Alfa and the other landowners will want your easement agreement to state how the owners will make decisions about the easement, but they likely don't want to evaluate these factors or undertake any other complicated process to decide who pays how much for each repair.

Instead, you can propose any of several alternatives to allocate costs. The first and easiest is to say that everyone will maintain the portion of the driveway on their own tract:

> XI. Each Owner will keep the portion of the Easement Area on that Owner's Tract in good order and repair.

If you propose that method, you will hear two objections from the owners. The first objection is that if the driveway is paved, then it's inefficient and expensive for each owner to decide when to repave or resurface the portion of the driveway on that owner's property. It's much more sensible to resurface the entire driveway at once instead of leaving the decision up to each owner separately. The second objection, which will come from everyone but Echo, is that Echo will get a free ride, because none of the common driveway is on Echo's property and thus Echo will not have to maintain anything.

---

[11]Freeman v. Sorchych, 226 Ariz. 242, 245 P.3d 927 (Ariz. App. 2011).

You then propose a second alternative that is almost as straightforward: the five users will each pay an equal share of the cost to maintain and repair the driveway.

> XI. The owners of the Alfa Tract, the Bravo Tract, the Charlie Tract, the Delta Tract, and the Echo Tract will each pay an equal share of the cost to maintain and repair the Easement Area.

When you propose this method, Alfa may point out that Alfa uses only a small portion of the driveway, Echo uses all of it, and Delta uses almost all of it, so why should Alfa pay as much as Delta and Echo? As you represent Alfa, you propose that the owners pay in proportion to the length of driveway that they use. Alfa uses one segment, Bravo uses two segments, Charlie uses three segments, and Delta and Echo each use four segments. Accordingly, Alfa will pay 1/14 of the cost, Bravo will pay 2/14, Charlie will pay 3/14, and Delta and Echo will each pay 4/14.

> XI. The Owners of the Tracts will pay the cost to maintain and repair the Easement Area in the following proportions:

Alfa Tract	1/14
Bravo Tract	2/14
Charlie Tract	3/14
Delta Tract	4/14
Echo Tract	4/14

A group of five owners will have at least one purist who will point out that the landowners don't use all of the driveway that's on their property, but have private driveways that split off from the common driveway at some point inside their property, not (as the preceding formula would have it) at the east line of their property. If the connection points for Alfa, Bravo, Charlie, and Delta are all at the midpoint of the portion of the driveway on their property, then the proportions in which they will share the costs become 1/24, 3/24, 5/24, 7/24, and 8/24. They could even go out with a tape measure or scale a line on an aerial photograph to allocate the costs more exactly than that. All I can advise you here is that they will ultimately be more content to have a simple formula that is not exactly accurate than to argue their way to an accurate formula that is not simple.

5.6.2 Recording the Easement Effectively

You and your client want the easement agreement to bind and benefit future owners. When the parties have signed and acknowledged the easement agreement, you will want to record it.

You also want to make the easement agreement easy for title insurers and abstractors to find by making it clear on the first page who the parties are (for the county's assistance in indexing the names) and by making it clear what properties are affected, so that title plants can put the recorded easement agreement in the electronic equivalent of the right lot book.

I handle the first goal by putting indexing information at the top of the first page or on a separate cover sheet, and by capitalizing the words in the name that I want the county indexer to use. If the agreement is conveying an easement from John P. Smith to Mary Q. Jones, I will have something like this at the top left of the first page:

Easement Agreement

Grantor:	SMITH, John P. [address]
Grantee:	JONES, Mary Q. [address]

I've made it clear to the reader that I want this agreement to be indexed under the names of Smith and Jones. For the convenience of the local title plant, I may also have a general reference in the header to where the subject property is, such as:

Affects: Land in the NW quarter of Section 12, T1S, R3E, W.M.[12]

Or, if the land is in a subdivision, I might write:

Affects: Part of Lots 12, 13, and 14, ASPHALT HEIGHTS

[12] The "W.M." stands for "Willamette Meridian," which is the reference meridian for Oregon and Washington.

I would include the "Affects" reference even if my easement agreement is not covering all of Section 12, or in the case of the second example, all of Lots 12, 13, and 14, because the legal descriptions in or attached to the agreement will state exactly what parcels or lots the easement agreement affects.

5.6.3 Disclaim a Dedication to the Public

If you are writing an easement agreement between private landowners then I strongly recommend that you include a disclaimer of any intent to dedicate any interest to the public or to any other person:

> 8. The Parties are making this Agreement for their exclusive benefit and not with the intent to create any rights in third parties or in the public. There are no third-party beneficiaries of this Agreement, and no person other than the Parties or their successors in interest in the Grantor Tract and the Grantee Tract will have any right to enforce this Agreement.

If the parties are making the easement agreement for the benefit of a third party, then you should identify the third party, or—better yet—make the third party a party to the agreement.

6
Appurtenant Utility Easements

6.1 Differences Between Utility Easements in Gross and Appurtenant Utility Easements

As discussed in sections 3.1 and 3.2, many utility easements are easements in gross: they are easements to a utility company for lines or pipes that will be part of a larger network, not installed to benefit a particular property. Property owners do sometimes give easements to neighbors for utility lines to benefit a particular property, and those easements are appurtenant to the benefited property.

Property owners also sometimes give easements to a utility company for the benefit of a particular property, not for the utility network generally. Are those easements appurtenant to the property or are they easements in gross?

An appurtenant easement is given to the owner of a tract of land for the benefit of that tract of land. If I give you an easement to install a power line across my property to serve your house, the easement is appurtenant to your property. When you sell your property, your rights in the easement pass to the next buyer. It's not so simple if I give an easement to our local utility, Good Neighbor Power Company, so that Good Neighbor can run a line to your house. The easement isn't appurtenant to any property that Good Neighbor owns, but it's not clearly an easement in gross either because it isn't for the general benefit of Good Neighbor to help Good Neighbor serve its customers in the area; it's to allow Good Neighbor to serve one specific customer, you.[1] If your jurisdiction still follows the Ackroyd rule (see section 2.2) and holds that easements in gross are not transferable, what happens when the power company sells its system to another company? Does the power company's easement terminate?

Power companies have been fairly stable. Not so with telephone companies.[2] Why tempt fate? Grant the easement not to the utility company but to the adjoining property owner, and allow the easement holder to give permission to utility companies to install the poles and connect the wires.

6.2 If Your Easement Is Appurtenant, Identify It as Appurtenant

The law presumes that easements are appurtenant to particular benefited properties unless the easement agreement states that the parties are creating an easement in gross, or unless the easement agreement can't possibly be creating an easement appurtenant to any particular property. If you grant an easement to an oil company to install a pipeline across your property in Kansas to connect an oilfield in North Dakota with a refinery in Texas, not even the hardiest of purists would argue that the easement is appurtenant to the Texas refinery instead of being an easement in gross to the oil company.

The difference is important because appurtenant easements pass with the land and bind and benefit the parties' successors in interest, but at common law easements in gross were not assignable. The question of whether the easement survives the sale of the property that the easement serves may depend on whether the court interprets the easement as an appurtenant easement or an easement in gross.

---

1 A law professor who has read to this point will mutter that you can't create an appurtenant easement by conveying an easement right to an entity that doesn't have any rights in the benefited property. I would agree, except that I've seen it done.

2 In the twenty-five years that my wife and I have owned our house, four different companies have owned the local telephone wires.

Don't let the court determine what your clients intended: make their intent clear in the document. For example, you could write:

> 1. Grantor grants to Grantee, for the benefit of and appurtenant to the Grantee Tract, a perpetual non-exclusive easement to lay down, maintain, repair, and replace an underground sanitary sewer line beneath that portion of the Grantor Tract legally described on the attached Exhibit C and depicted on the attached Exhibit D (that portion the "Easement Area"), on the conditions of this Agreement.

No court will mistake that clause as creating an easement in gross.

6.3 Can the Burdened Property Connect to the Utility Line?

The grantee is going to install utility lines across the Grantor Tract to serve the Grantee Tract. You or your client should consider whether the grantor can use the same lines, both legally and physically.

In the simple example shown in Figure 6.1, the owner of the Grantee Tract wants an easement to run a driveway along the north side of the Grantor Tract, and to install utility poles to bring an overhead power line and an overhead phone line from a nearby public

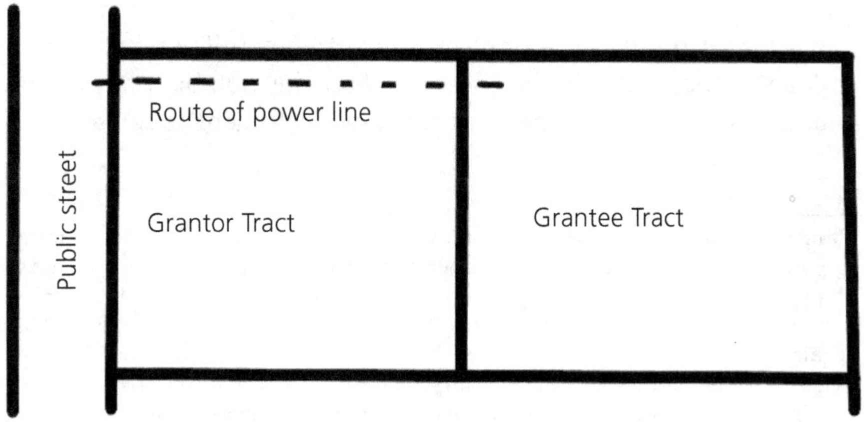

Figure 6.1 They'll share the driveway. Will they share the power line and poles?

street to serve a house that the grantee intends to build on the Grantee Tract. The Grantor Tract is vacant.

Other sections of the easement agreement cover where the driveway will cross the Grantor Tract to get from the street to the Grantee Tract. Because the grantor can use the easement area in any way that doesn't unreasonably interfere with the grantee's use, we know that the grantor can use the driveway that the grantee will build in common with the grantee. When the grantor builds a house on the Grantor Tract, the grantor will need to run a power line and a phone line to the house. Can the grantor string the grantor's lines on the grantee's utility poles?

The question is interesting. On the one hand, it's a principle of easement law that unless the easement agreement prohibits the grantor from using the easement area, the grantor can use the easement area in any way that doesn't unreasonably interfere with the grantee's exercise of the grantee's easement rights. The grantor could string lines on the grantee's poles without interfering with the power and phone service to the grantee's house. The grantee might not even notice or care.

On the other hand, the easement area belongs to the grantor, but the poles themselves belong to the grantee, who paid to install them. The grantee might say that the grantor is free to erect a second set of utility poles but can't use the grantee's poles without paying the grantee for that right.[3]

If you represent the grantor, instead of leaving this question to chance you can cover it in your easement agreement, perhaps as follows:

> 4. Grantor reserves the right to attach to any utility poles that Grantee may install in the Easement Area any number of power and communications lines and ancillary equipment to serve the Grantor Tract.[4]

---

[3] It may seem odd to you that the grantor would have to pay for permission to install a power line on the grantor's own property, but people get quirky when it comes to property rights, and will often spend vast sums to litigate over very small stakes.

[4] The power company may install a step-down transformer, a power meter, or other equipment on the poles where the line leaves the pole to serve the grantor's house. The telephone and cable companies may want to install junction boxes or other equipment where their lines leave the pole to run to the grantor's house. If you draft the agreement to allow the grantor to install only lines, an unreasonable grantee may object to the utility companies installing anything other than actual lines on the grantee's poles.

If the grantee responds that the grantor shouldn't be able to use the grantee's expensive utility poles free of charge, you might respond by adding a cost-sharing provision to the clause.

> 4. Grantor reserves the right to attach to any utility poles that Grantee may install in the Easement Area power and communications lines to serve the Grantor Tract. If Grantor installs power or communications lines on Grantee's utility poles, then Grantor will reimburse Grantee for one-half of Grantee's cost to install the poles in the Easement Area, which Grantee will provide to Grantor when Grantee installs the poles.

If your client is granting an easement for a sanitary sewer line to run from the Grantee Tract west to the street, then you must consider gravity. Power and phone lines care little for elevation and can be increased in capacity by stringing another line. A public water line can run uphill or downhill. Sewerage, however, flows downhill. Will the grantee install a sewer line that is large enough to handle the sewerage from a future house on the Grantor Tract as well as that from the house on the Grantee Tract, and will the line be deep enough for the grantor to be able to connect without installing a pump? If your jurisdiction does not allow two tracts to share a single sewer connection, then your issue is different: will the grantee install the sewer line in a location and at a depth that won't block your client's eventual connection to the public sewer line? You can recommend that your grantor client consult a civil engineer to evaluate the grantee's plan for underground utilities and confirm that the grantee's underground lines won't conflict with how your client will someday connect to the public system.

7
Party Walls

A party wall is a wall built on the line between two parcels that is intended to support the structures on both parcels. They were common in urban commercial areas, when adjoining landowners might agree to build a single wall on the lot line instead of each building separate and adjoining walls. Each would then build his or her separate building, using the party wall as a structural element.

Those with diligent counsel would sign and record a party wall agreement in which each owner agreed to pay half the cost to maintain the wall in good condition and not to damage the wall or alter it in a way that would impair its support of the two buildings. The party wall agreement granted each owner the right to maintain and repair the half of the wall that was on the other parcel, including the right to enter the other parcel when necessary to repair the wall. The party wall agreement granted reciprocal easements, even if it didn't use the word "easement."

The people who created party walls 100 or more years ago didn't much think about the problems that would arise if an owner wanted to add on to the party wall to support more floors, or to take the party wall down and redevelop a property. Both raising and razing party walls present practical problems, which may be why adjoining owners don't often create new party walls today.

Party wall agreements remain relevant to the practitioner in at least two contexts today. First is when your client buys property subject to a party wall agreement and wants to negotiate changes with the adjoining owner. Second is when a developer of a single large parcel intends to build and sell townhomes that will be a single structure that will straddle one lot for each unit, but not be a condominium or cooperative.

7.1 History of Party Walls

Why did adjoining owners agree to build party walls instead of constructing separate walls? One reason was cost: building a single wall would be more expensive than building two separate walls at different times, but not twice as expensive. Another reason was space: a party wall is no wider than a single wall. Adjoining owners of lots 100 feet wide might not care, but adjoining owners of lots that are only twenty-five feet wide would value even an extra six inches or a foot of interior space that they might gain from sharing in a party wall. Party walls became common in areas with narrow lots, such as lower Manhattan, where the lots were often twenty-five feet wide or less.[1] The benefit to the owners was significant: The interior space in a building with party walls on both sides could be sixteen inches wider than in a building without party walls—not significant for a building on a 100-foot-wide lot, but valuable in a building on a twenty-two-foot-wide lot.

Early party wall agreements often omitted to cover two important points. First, could either owner extend the party wall upward over both tracts, or could either owner use the space above that owner's portion of the party wall for a separate non–party wall? Second, what can an owner who wants to demolish a building and redevelop the lot do with the party wall that's shared with the neighbor?

7.1.1 Party Wall Litigation

Reported litigation on party walls dates back to a decision of the English Court of Common Pleas in *Matts v. Hawkins*, 5 Taunton 20

[1] For example, the 1879 Bromley Atlas of New York shows that block fronts on Third Avenue near 10th Street, two hundred feet long, typically had nine, sometimes ten, different lots, for an average lot width of only twenty to twenty-two feet.

(1813). Twenty-five years earlier, adjoining owners had built a party wall, each paying half the cost. About ten years before the case was decided, Hawkins demolished his building, leaving the party wall standing. Hawkins then built a shed against the party wall. Some years later Matts, whose building still stood, began to extend the party wall upward to support another floor. Hawkins tore down the extension, and then when Matts started to rebuild it, Hawkins tore it down again. The issue was whether each owner owned the half of the wall that was on his property, or whether they were tenants in common in the entire wall. Hawkins argued that he and Matts were tenants in common in the entire wall, and that Matts could not maintain a trespass claim against a tenant in common.

The court rejected Hawkins's argument. The court held that Matts and Hawkins were not tenants in common as to the wall, but each enjoyed certain rights in the portion of the wall on the other's property, which Judge Gibbs characterized as "easements."[2]

New York courts have followed *Matts*[3] and treated the rights of party wall owners as reciprocal easement rights, whether or not the word "easement" appears in the party wall agreement.

An 1895 Pennsylvania statute authorized landowners to remove the walls of their neighbors and replace them with party walls, under a procedure that required notice to the adjoining owner, followed by a government inspection and approval. A theater's side wall was built on the property line. The city approved the neighbor's request to build a party wall to support a new fifteen-floor department store,[4] and permitted the neighbor to demolish the theater's wall and replace it with a party wall. The theater owner sued for damages, including the loss of rental income for one theater season. The theater owner also alleged that by giving his neighbor the right to build a party wall on the theater property, the Pennsylvania party wall statute unconstitutionally deprived him of an interest in his property.

---

[2] Matts v. Hawkins, 5 Taunton at 24.

[3] American cases that cite *Matts* sometimes misspell the case name as "Watt" or "Watts." *E.g.*, Brooks v. Curtis, 50 N.Y. 639 (1873), *Den ex dem.* Richman v. Baldwin, 21 N.J.L. 395 (N.J. Sup. Ct. 1848).

[4] Nathan Isaacs, *Statutory Party Walls*, 71 U. Pa. L. Rev. 229 (1923). This article describes the history of party wall statutes and case law in other states, including Iowa, Massachusetts, Mississippi, and South Carolina.

The case made it to the United States Supreme Court as *Jackman v. Rosenbaum Co.*, 260 U.S. 22 (1922). Justice Holmes, writing for a unanimous court, said that "the custom of party walls was introduced by the first settlers in Philadelphia under William Penn, and has prevailed in the state ever since," noting that Pennsylvania had adopted party wall statutes for Philadelphia in 1721 and for Pittsburgh in 1794. Holmes said that as the easement for a potential party wall had been an encumbrance on Pennsylvania property for so many years, and was "steeped in local tradition," the Supreme Court should not overrule the practice on Fourteenth Amendment grounds. Since then, the Supreme Court has left litigation over party walls to the lower courts and to the states.

7.1.2 Legislation

Pennsylvania's statute authorizing cities to regulate party walls remains in force.[5] Other states have adopted laws to authorize party walls.[6] If your state has a party wall statute, or if the city where the property is located has a party wall ordinance, review the statute or ordinance before you begin to draft the easement agreement.

7.2 Reviewing a Party Wall Agreement

Your client is buying property and the title report shows an exception for a recorded party wall agreement. Here are my recommendations for what you should do.

First, see if the party wall is still in place. If the party wall agreement was recorded in 1878 and the two buildings now standing were built in 1948 and 1973, the wall may be long gone. If the wall no longer stands, then the party wall agreement has become obsolete. Propose that the seller and the adjoining owner record an agreement that terminates the party wall agreement. Both should be motivated to remove an encumbrance on their title that benefits neither of them.

If the party wall no longer stands but the adjoining owner is immune to your blandishments, ask your client's title insurer to

---

5 11 Pa. C.S. § 12413.

6 *Statutory Party Walls*, 71 U. Pa. L. Rev. at 230–33.

exclude the party wall agreement from the title policy and insist that the deed from the seller not list the party wall agreement as an exception. The title company may refuse to remove the party wall agreement as an exception on the title report, meaning that the title company will not defend your client if the adjoining owner sues to reestablish a party wall, but your client's deed will not be evidence that your client accepted the obsolete party wall agreement as an exception to title.

If the party wall is still standing and in use, check the agreement for three things:

- Can either party extend the wall upward, and if so, on just that party's property or on both halves of the wall?
- How do the parties agree on maintaining and repairing the wall when necessary?
- What happens to the agreement if one owner demolishes his or her building?

A party wall agreement may contain an express limitation on the height of the wall. If it does not expressly limit the height of the wall or prohibit the owners from independently extending the wall upward, but does describe the wall as being of a certain height or as constructed to support adjacent buildings of a specified number of floors, a court may interpret the statement of building height as a limitation on the height of the wall.[7]

---

[7] *See, e.g.*, Henne v. Lankershim, 146 Cal. 70, 79 P. 591 (1905). Henne and Lankershim owned adjoining buildings in Los Angeles and shared a party wall under a written agreement that stated that the wall was to be five stories tall. Lankershim wanted to extend the wall upward to support two more floors. Henne objected. The California supreme court held that the statement in the agreement that the wall was for a five-floor building operated as a limit on its height, and Lankershim could not extend the party wall upward, even on his own property, without the consent of Henne. The *Lankershim* court, relying on precedent, said "where the agreement is for a party wall of a designated height, the designation of the height is, in the absence of other provisions, a limitation, beyond which neither party can go without the consent of the other. The agreement constitutes a conveyance of the easement to that height, and no more." *Henne v. Lankershim,* 146 Cal. at 72.

7.3 Drafting a Party Wall Agreement

If your client wants to buy a property with a party wall that has no party wall agreement, recommend that your client negotiate a party wall agreement with the adjoining owner as a condition to closing, so that the agreement will be in place when your client takes title. Reduce the chance that your client's name becomes attached to the lead party-wall case of the twenty-first century.

One convenience of drafting an agreement for a wall that already exists is that you know what you're allowing. You can see it and have it measured and surveyed. You can also ask the seller and the neighbor how they maintain the party wall, and if they have had any disagreements about the party wall.

The place to start is by asking your client and the neighbor about the three points I mentioned in section 7.2. Do they want to be able to extend the wall upward, and if so, on one or both properties? How do they agree on maintenance and repair? What happens if one building is demolished or destroyed? With the answers to those questions in hand, you can start drafting the easement agreement.

7.3.1 Begin With the Recitals

Begin with the recitals that explain why the parties are making the agreement.[8] The recitals in a party wall agreement for an existing wall might look like this:

RECITALS

A. South Owner[9] owns Lots 7 and 8, Block 4, OCKHAMS ADDITION, in Archaic County, Massachusetts (the "South Tract"). The South Tract is improved with a building (the "South Building") currently addressed as 77 Ockhams Razor Way, Archaicville, Massachusetts.

B. North Owner owns Lots 9 and 10, Block 4, OCKHAMS ADDITION, in Archaic County, Massachusetts (the "North

---

[8] I include recitals in most of my negotiated contracts to explain to future readers why the parties made this contract and to state the facts on which they were relying.

[9] You will have defined the parties as "South Owner" and "North Owner" in the preamble to the agreement.

Tract"). The North Tract is improved with a building (the "North Building") currently addressed as 79 Ockhams Razor Way, Archaicville, Massachusetts.

C. The South Building and the North Building each include a basement, a ground floor at street level, and two upper floors.
D. The North Tract is adjacent to and north of the South Tract. The south line of Lot 9 is the north line of Lot 8.
E. For many years a party wall has stood along the line between Lot 8 and Lot 9 and has supported the South Building and the North Building. Half of the party wall is on Lot 8 and half is on Lot 9.
F. South Owner and North Owner wish to set down in writing their agreement on maintaining, repairing, and replacing the party wall.

These recitals explain why the parties are making this agreement. Having explained why the parties are making the agreement, continue to the body of the agreement itself.

7.3.2 Grant the Reciprocal Easements

Next, think back on *Matts v. Hawkins* and whether you want to cast the party wall agreement in the form of a reciprocal easement agreement. Assuming that you do, here is how you might start the agreement portion:

NOW, THEREFORE, SOUTH OWNER AND NORTH OWNER AGREE:

1. The recitals above are true and correct and are part of this Agreement.
2. In consideration of South Owner entering into this Agreement, North Owner grants to South Owner a permanent easement over the South 2.50 feet[10] of the North Tract to use, maintain, [and repair] [repair, and replace] the party wall described in the recitals to this Agreement, for the support of the South Building.

---

[10] Adjust the dimension as necessary to match what exists.

3. In consideration of North Owner entering into this Agreement, South Owner grants to North Owner a permanent easement over the North 2.50 feet of the South Tract to use, maintain, [and repair] [repair, and replace] the party wall described in the recitals to this Agreement, for the Support of the North Building.

7.3.3 To Add or Not to Add? That Is the First Question

Do the parties want to add on to the wall and make their buildings taller in the future? Or do they want the wall to stay no higher than it is now? Here are two alternate provisions to cover that point:

VI. The party wall currently extends approximately ___ feet above the grade of the adjoining public street, Ockhams Razor Way. If either party wishes to add [one additional floor] [one or more additional floors] to that party's building, the party may extend the party wall upward as necessary to enclose and support the additional floor[s]. The party that extends the wall [may build up to one-half of the width of the wall extension on the portion of the other party's Tract subject to the party wall easement] [must build the extension, if at all, only on that party's Tract and not on the Tract of the other party].

Or, if both owners are willing to agree not to extend the wall upward, they can include a clause like the following:

VI. The party wall currently extends approximately ___ feet above the grade of the adjoining public street, Ockhams Razor Way. Neither party may extend the party wall above its current height or use the party wall to support an additional floor on that party's building.

7.3.4 Repairs and Maintenance

Every easement agreement should assign the responsibility to maintain the improvements in the easement area. Party walls are no exception. If you do not assign the responsibility to maintain the wall, a court or legislature may some day do it for you.

You can use this simple maintenance provision to share the cost of repairs and maintenance equally between the adjoining owners:

> VII. The North Owner and the South Owner will each pay one-half of the cost to maintain the party wall in good condition, and to repair any damage to the party wall.

More sophisticated or wary owners, or owners with unequal bargaining power, may want the agreement to describe how the parties will determine whether repairs are necessary—one owner may want to maintain the wall in first-class condition and the other may be satisfied with "good enough." One may want to perform preventative maintenance and the other may not want to spend any money until something needs to be repaired. Here is a more complex maintenance clause:

> VII. The North Owner and the South Owner will each pay one-half the cost to maintain the party wall in good condition, and to repair any damage to the party wall. If either owner believes that the party wall is in need of repair, that owner will solicit bids for the repair work from licensed and reputable contractors and will present them to the other owner for review and approval. The owners may agree to accept one of the bids. If the owners do not agree to accept one of the bids, or if the owners do not agree that repairs are necessary, then either owner may submit the question to be determined under the dispute resolution provisions of Section ___ of this Agreement.

You can include a provision for the owners to have the wall evaluated by a structural engineer, who will then recommend repairs for the owners to consider:

> VII. In odd-numbered years, the owners will engage a licensed and experienced structural engineering firm to inspect and evaluate the party wall, to report on its condition, and to describe any maintenance or repairs that the engineering firm may recommend. The owners will each pay one-half the fees of the engineering firm and will carry out the recommended

maintenance or repairs unless both owners agree not to have the work performed. The owners will each pay one-half the cost of the maintenance or repairs that the engineering firm recommends, and of any other repair work that is necessitated by casualty or emergency.

In deciding how much detail to include in the clause on maintenance and repairs, keep in mind that a reciprocal party wall easement differs from an ordinary access easement. In a one-way access easement, one party is using the property of the other party. They have no common interest. The burdened party may be happy to have the easement holder cease to maintain the easement improvements because the easement holder may eventually give up using the easement altogether. In a party wall easement, however, each party wants to maintain the wall to support that party's building. Neither party wants the buildings to fall, and they are less likely to get into arguments over maintenance and repairs than are the holders of easements for private driveways.

7.3.5 Demolition and Reconstruction

Easements last forever, unless you write them to terminate. Buildings last a very long time, but not forever. If you are writing a party wall agreement for an existing wall, discuss with the property owners what should happen if both buildings are demolished, or if only one is demolished.

The simple answer if both buildings are demolished is to provide that when the owners rebuild, each will build foundations and side walls entirely on their property, and not replace the party wall with a new party wall. Whether that answer is practicable depends on topography and lot size. If the party wall separates two lots that are 100 feet wide, each owner has plenty of room to rebuild while keeping the foundation and side wall entirely on that owner's property. But if the lots are thirty feet wide or less, each owner would lose a lot of floor space if each had to build a separate replacement wall.

If the owners would replace the party wall with a new party wall, start with this provision:

VII. If the North Building and the South Building are both demolished or destroyed, then the North Owner and the

South Owner will replace the party wall with a new party wall designed and built to be capable of supporting buildings on the North Tract and the South Tract of up to ___ floors above ground. The party that replaces its building first (in this section, the "Building Party") will pay the cost to build the party wall and furnish an accounting of the cost to the other party. The second party will reimburse the Building Party for one-half the cost to build the party wall before the second party begins construction on the second party's building. The second party will reimburse the Building Party for one-half the cost to build the party wall whether the second party uses all or part of the party wall.

The last sentence of this clause forestalls a second party who builds a shorter or shallower building from trying to pay less than half the cost on the ground that the second building is using less than the wall's full height or length.

It's more complicated to handle the situation of one building being demolished, whether intentionally for redevelopment or by casualty. The owner of the now-vacant lot may want to rely on a new side wall instead of the old party wall; the owner of the other lot will want to keep the old wall in place. If the parties are agreeing that the wall will stay in place, you can start with a clause like this one:

VII. If the building on one Tract is demolished or destroyed, whether intentionally or by a casualty, the owner of that Tract will repair any damage to the party wall that resulted from the demolition or destruction, at that owner's sole expense, so that the party wall continues to provide adequate support to the building on the other Tract.

You could provide the opposite: that if one building is demolished or destroyed then the other owner has a limited time, perhaps two years, to provide support for the surviving building on the other owner's own property. This seems to me to be an unsatisfactory resolution. If prospective lenders on the two properties understand that the party wall agreement imposes on their borrowers not just the ordinary duty to maintain the wall in good repair but, under certain circumstances, to make a substantial structural alteration because the other owner decides to demolish the neighboring building, they may be reluctant to finance or refinance the properties. You are writing party wall agreements and other easements not just for your client, the other party, and future owners of the tracts, but also for future lenders. Don't give your client a spectacular agreement that scares lenders from financing whomever your client will eventually sell to.

8
View Easements

8.1 General Principles of View Easements

The classic easement is a landowner's grant to another of a right to enter on the grantor's property, either simply to cross the grantor's property (for example, the right to use an existing driveway or parking area) or, in addition, to construct improvements on the grantor's property (for example, a powerline or pipeline easement). The classic definition of an easement was stretched when negative covenants to protect views and access to sunlight began to be expressed as easements.

The concept of a negative covenant is simple: Grantor promises to Grantee that Grantor and Grantor's successors will not put the Grantor's land to certain uses; for instance, that the Grantor will not allow trees to grow above the height at which they would block a specified view from the Grantee's property.

The negative covenant is not a classic easement, because the Grantee does not receive any general right to enter the Grantor's property or to construct improvements on the Grantor's property. The right to enjoy a view over a neighbor's property without entering the property isn't a right to enter the neighbor's property itself. The Grantee might have the conditional right only to enter to correct a violation—to cut down an offending tree if the Grantor refused to cut the tree.

Today, lawyers (including me) are deaf to the plaintive cries of the classicists, and we insouciantly label as a "View Easement" the document that we draft to protect our client's view over a neighboring property. This chapter will describe how to design and draft a view easement. I'll use as my example homeowners named Overton who want to protect their view of Mount Hood across the property of their neighbors, the Underhills. The Underhills are willing, for a fee, to grant the Overtons a view easement over the Underhill tract for the benefit of the house on the Overtons' property.

8.2 Identify the View to Be Protected

The first step is to identify the view to be protected. It doesn't work to protect "the view from the Overton Tract" without identifying what that view is. You can stand on the Overton Tract, or look out the windows of the Overtons' house, and see many things, only some of which lie beyond the Underhills' property and only some of which may be practical to protect.

In our example, the Overtons tell you that they want to buy a view easement "to protect our view of Mount Hood." The view from where? It may be possible to see Mount Hood from many points on their property. They may be most concerned, however, with the view from the living room, the master bedroom, and a particular deck.

Visit the Overtons' house and look at the views for yourself. If you cannot visit, then ask the Overtons to send you photographs of the views from the points they wish to protect, and work out on a map or aerial photograph that the views do in fact pass over the Underhills' property. Your best work won't do the Overtons any good if it turns out that they should have been negotiating with the Brandybucks instead of with the Underhills.

You now have a basis from which to define the easement and the easement area.

8.3 Defining the Easement Area

Now that you know which views the Overtons want to protect, you can begin to define the easement area. Only rarely will the easement area include the entire Underhill tract, unless the Underhill tract is downhill from the Overton tract and entirely within the view corridor the Overtons want to protect. Usually there will be some swath of the Underhill tract that's essential to the view, and usually there will be some use of that swath that will remain allowable: perhaps a one-floor house in the swath won't block the Overtons' view, but a two-floor house might. You thus have to determine an area (the swath) and a height limit (an elevation).

You can roughly determine the area by working from an aerial photograph of the Overton and Underhill tracts, drawing lines that represent the swath (the horizontal limits of the view to be protected), and then superimposing those lines on a tax map or survey of the area. To avoid misunderstandings and litigation in the future, you will want to translate those lines into a legal description of a portion of the Underhill tract. If you are fortunate your description might be as simple as "the South 10 feet of the Grantor Tract." If your swath (the view corridor) runs through the middle of the Underhill tract then you can convert your lines into a legal description. By "you" I actually mean the surveyor that you will encourage the Overtons to hire to draft the legal description.[1]

If you don't have a recent elevation survey of the Overtons' tract or of the adjoining street, you will also want the surveyor's advice in determining the elevation that will be the floor of the view easement. You can define the floor of the view corridor in one of three ways. One way is to define it as a certain distance above ground level, for instance as "twelve feet above the existing ground level of the Easement Area." The floor of the view corridor will slope up and down with the ground beneath—and it will change if the Underhills alter the ground.

A second way to define the floor of the view corridor is as a fixed elevation. If your friendly surveyor tells you that the Overtons' deck is 366 feet above sea level, then you may define the floor of the view corridor as being a fixed elevation that you and the Overtons pick in relation to the deck level. For example, their view of Mount Hood

[1] In many states, as a licensed attorney you can draft a legal description without also holding a license as a surveyor or engineer, but your license doesn't assure you and the Overtons that you can draft it competently or that you can detect errors in the legal descriptions in the recorded documents on which you would have to rely.

might not be blocked by anything on the Underhill tract that's no more than four feet above the deck level. You could then describe the floor of the easement area as "bounded by a horizontal plane that is 370 feet above sea level." If you define the view corridor floor by a fixed elevation, then you should also state what that elevation is based on—over the past century there have been three or four definitions of "sea level" in the United States, all different. Your surveyor can help here too, perhaps by giving you language that sounds like this: "The elevations in this Agreement and on the attached map are based on Datum ____________" or " . . . are based on the elevation of the sidewalk in front of the Grantor Tract being at an elevation of X feet."

8.4 Are You Prohibiting All Structures or Only Those Above a Certain Height?

If you have drafted your easement agreement well, any reader will be able to tell whether it prohibits all structures or only those above a certain height. After you write your provision, read it and look for ambiguities, loopholes, and modifiers so that your client does not end up in the situation of the property owner and easement holder in a 2018 Massachusetts case.[2]

In that case, the plaintiff held a view easement over adjoining land on Nantucket Island. The deed for the burdened land stated that it was subject to

> * * * a permanent and non-exclusive view easement which prohibits any and all structures and/or vegetation with a height greater than eight (8′) feet from existing grade upon and over said Lot.

Both parties argued to the trial court that the easement language was unambiguous. The plaintiffs (the easement holders) argued that this clause unambiguously prohibited construction of any and all structures, and that the language allowed vegetation up to eight feet

[2] MacLean v. Conservation Commission of Nantucket, No. 17-P-746, Memorandum and Order (Mass. App. 2018). The real party in interest was not the Conservation Commission but a company called Oak Hill Investments, LLC, the owner of the burdened lot.

high. The defendants (owners of the burdened property) argued that this clause unambiguously allowed both structures and vegetation, as long as they did not exceed eight feet in height.

The property owners wanted to build a deck and a staircase, both below eight feet in height. The easement holders sued to enforce the agreement.

The trial court agreed with the property owners. The court held that the eight-foot limit unambiguously applied to both structures and vegetation, and that the property owners could build a deck and staircase that were less than eight feet in height. The easement holders appealed.

The court of appeals reversed the trial court and found the language to be ambiguous. In the court's words, "the absence of a comma after the word 'structures' combined with the use of the term 'and/or' makes it unclear whether the eight-foot height restriction applies only to vegetation or to structures as well."

That was an expensive missing comma.

Here is how the drafter of that clause could have written it to state that the property owner could build structures up to eight feet tall and allow vegetation to grow up to eight feet tall:

> * * * a permanent and non-exclusive view easement which prohibits any structures and vegetation from exceeding eight (8) feet in height above existing grade upon and over said Lot.

If, however, the drafter had wanted to prohibit all structures, but to allow vegetation up to eight feet high, the drafter could have revised that clause to read like this:

> * * * a permanent and non-exclusive view easement which prohibits:
> (a) any and all structures upon and over said Lot, and
> (b) any vegetation with a height greater than eight (8) feet from existing grade upon and over said Lot.

Don't be bashful about using numbered and bulleted lists in your easement agreements to make it clear whether a height restriction applies to structures, to trees, or to both.

8.5 Granting the View Easement

Here is how you might word the granting clause in an agreement that creates a view easement in a portion of the airspace of the Grantor Tract:

> 2. Grantor grants to Grantee, for the benefit of and appurtenant to the Grantee Tract, a permanent view easement over and through that certain portion of the airspace above the Grantor Tract (the "View Easement Area") that is 370 feet above Sea Level[3] or higher.

You might alternatively define the View Easement Area to be bounded by a plane or planes, as follows:

> 2. Grantor grants to Grantee, for the benefit of and appurtenant to the Grantee Tract, a permanent view easement over and through that certain portion of the airspace above the Grantor Tract (the "View Easement Area") that is bounded on its sides by vertical planes extended upward from the lot lines of the Grantor Tract and that has as its lower bound a horizontal plane 370 feet above Sea Level.

If the Grantee is buying the right to prevent the Grantor from building anything on the surface of a portion of the Grantor Tract, then you don't need to define the lower bound of the View Easement Area to be a plane. You can define it to be the surface:

> 2. Grantor grants to Grantee, for the benefit of and appurtenant to the Grantee Tract, a permanent view easement over and through that certain portion of the Grantor Tract (the "View Easement Area") described on the attached Exhibit C and depicted on the attached Exhibit D.

---

[3] I'm assuming here that you've defined "Sea Level" with reference to a specific datum, or that you will define all elevations to be based on a known point near the property to be X feet above sea level, so that even if NOAA changes the datum, future owners will be able to calculate the elevation that the parties had in mind.

When you have defined the View Easement Area and granted the easement, you then continue by describing the rights that the grantor is giving the grantee with respect to the View Easement Area.[4] The grantor of a view easement will always give the grantee the right to prevent the grantor from constructing buildings that extend up into the View Easement Area, or, if the View Easement Area is a portion of the surface of the Grantor Tract, that exceed a specified height. Some view easements also give the grantee the right to enter the grantor's property to cut trees that grow into the View Easement Area.

Here is a clause that you could use to prohibit the Grantor from building anything in the View Easement Area if the View Easement Area is a chunk of airspace:

> 3. Grantor covenants to Grantee not to build or allow to be built any structure or improvement that extends into the View Easement Area.

If the View Easement Area goes down to the surface, then you could write the clause as follows:

> 3. Grantor covenants to Grantee not to build or allow to be built any structure or improvement [on or above the ground surface of the View Easement Area] [alternate: in the View Easement Area more than six feet in height above the ground surface].

8.6 What Remedies Will the Grantee Have If the Grantor Violates the Easement?

When you negotiate and draft a view easement, you have a ticklish problem that doesn't plague drafters of access easements and landscaping (boundary line) easements. If the grantor of an access easement interferes with the grantee's use of the easement, as for

[4] When you read these sample clauses, keep in mind that the "View Easement Area" is that portion of the Grantor Tract in which the Grantor won't construct anything, or in which the Grantor won't construct anything above a certain height. In some of these examples, the View Easement Area extends down to the surface of the Grantor Tract, and in other examples it doesn't.

instance by blocking the accessway, sometimes the grantee can simply unblock the accessway and resume using it. The parties to a landscaping easement usually have the easement area follow an existing fence line; the fence itself enforces the easement rights. In contrast, what does the grantee of a view easement do if the grantor lets trees grow into the view easement area?

At one end of the spectrum, the grantee can sue the grantor for injunctive relief, and ask the court to order the grantor to remove the obstruction. Litigation is slow and costly. If cases take two years to come to trial then the trees will be two years older, two years larger, and two years more expensive to top or remove by the time the judge rules.

At the other end of the spectrum, the easement agreement can give the grantee the right to enter the grantor's property to cut down and top or remove the encroaching trees. If you give the grantee the right to remove encroaching trees by self-help, require the grantee to notify the grantor first. Property owners react badly when awakened by unexpected chainsaws. You could include this provision:

> 6. If any trees or bushes grow into the View Easement Area and Grantor does not remove the encroaching portions of the trees or bushes within thirty days after Grantee notifies Grantor of the encroachment and requests Grantor to remove the encroaching portions, then Grantee may on five days' notice to Grantor enter the View Easement Area to cut and remove [the encroaching portions of the trees or bushes] [the trees and bushes in their entirety][, and Grantor will promptly reimburse Grantee for the expenses that Grantee incurs to remove the trees or bushes].

The laws of some states provide that the owner of trees or shrubs has a civil right of action against persons who cut or damage trees and shrubs without permission.[5] If your state law provides landowners with a civil right of action against persons who cut trees without

---

[5] Oregon's statute is ORS 105.810, which allows a landowner to recover treble damages against someone who willfully and without authority removes trees or shrubs from the landowner's property. California's similar statute is Cal. Civ. Code §3346. New York's statute is Real Property Actions §861.

permission, and if you are drafting the easement agreement to give the grantee the right of self-help, then include a statement that the grantor irrevocably authorizes the grantee to cut (or to cut and remove) the encroaching trees, and cite the statute to make it clear that if the grantee enters to cut and remove the encroaching trees, the grantee is cutting the trees with the permission of the grantor. In Oregon this provision could read:

> 6. If any trees or bushes grow into the View Easement Area and Grantor does not remove the encroaching portions of the trees or bushes within thirty days after Grantee notifies Grantor of the encroachment and requests Grantor to remove the encroaching portions, then Grantee may on five days' notice to Grantor enter the Grantor Tract and the View Easement Area to cut and remove [the encroaching portions of the trees or bushes] [the trees and bushes in their entirety][, and Grantor will promptly reimburse Grantee for the expenses that Grantee incurs to remove the trees or bushes]. Grantor irrevocably authorizes Grantee to enter the Grantor Tract to remove the encroaching trees and bushes from the View Easement Area and agrees that this Agreement gives Grantee "lawful authority"[6] to do so within the meaning of ORS 105.810.

---

[6] I'm quoting the exact words of Oregon's statute. Adjust the quotation as necessary to match the law of your state.

9
Encroachment Easements

To this point I've discussed agreements that contemplate a use that hasn't yet begun. This chapter covers encroachment easements, with special attention to easement agreements that are written to legitimize encroachments that already exist.

If you own a condominium unit, then your property is almost certainly subject to an encroachment easement. When condominium developers are ready to plat their projects they commonly include in the condominium declaration a provision like this one:

> Each Unit and all Common Elements shall have an easement over the other Units and all adjoining Common Elements for the purpose of accommodating any present or future encroachment as a result of engineering errors, construction, reconstruction, repairs, settlement, shifting, or other movement of any portion of the Property, or any other similar cause, and any encroachment due to building overhang or projection.

This provision states that if the actual location of the units and the common elements deviates slightly from the surveyed location as platted, or if the buildings shift and move so that some of the units slightly encroach into the airspace of other units, the improvements can remain where they are. If the condominium building settles by an inch, your downstairs neighbor cannot make you lift your unit up by an inch to remove it from the neighbor's platted airspace.

9.1 Encroachment Easements for Fence Lines

Let's move from urban condominiums to suburban neighborhoods. Smith and Jones own houses on adjoining half-acre lots. For many years, a fence has separated their yards, and Smith and Jones have treated the fence as their common property line. This year, Smith hired a surveyor, who reports that the fence crosses the property line: the west end of the fence is eighteen inches on Jones's side of the actual line, and the east end is twelve inches on Smith's side of the line. For years, as it turns out, Jones has been using a bit of the east end of Smith's property, and Smith has been using a bit of the west end of Jones's property (Figure 9.1).

What are Smith and Jones to do? They could agree to take down the fence and rebuild it on the actual property line, thus moving the fence to match the property line. More expensively, they could petition the local government to approve a boundary line adjustment, moving the property line to match the fence.

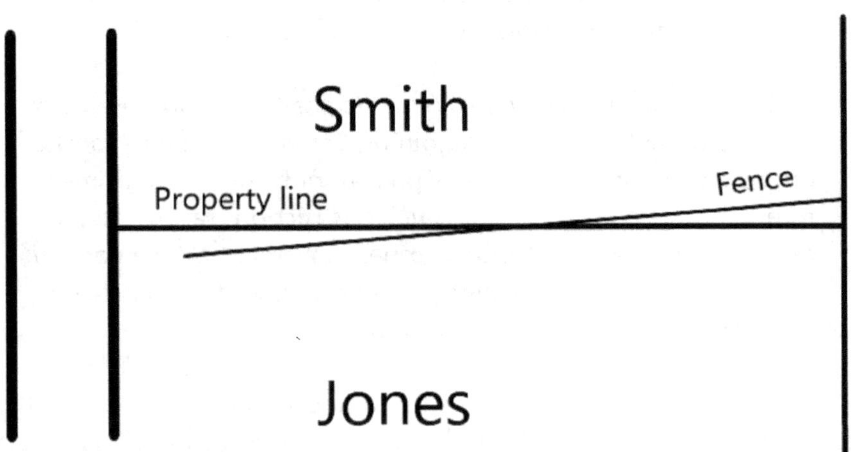

Figure 9.1 The fence doesn't follow the line: time for an encroachment easement?

Even more expensively still, they could sue each other, each claiming to have acquired title by adverse possession to the encroachment areas, taking the first step in what will become a neighborhood war of legend.

Which alternative will they choose?

The Smiths and Joneses in this situation rarely move the fence, either because they replaced the fence only a few years ago or because the new fence would run through Smith's azaleas and Jones's rose bushes, cutting off bits of the irrigation systems of both yards. They look into applying for a boundary line adjustment, an idea that they abandon when the city tells them what the application fee is and that they'll need the consent of their home mortgage lenders. They could sue each other, if they don't mind never speaking to each other again.

Smith and Jones have a fourth alternative, simpler and cheaper than the others. They can sign an encroachment easement agreement, in which each grants to the other the right to maintain and landscape the portion of the grantor's property that lies on the grantee's side of the fence. If they are each willing to take the small risk that a foreclosure by the other party's lender would extinguish the agreement, they can solve their problem faster and more cheaply than with any of the other alternatives, and without needing any government or lender approval.

As with most agreements, start by drafting the recitals—the paragraphs that tell the reader the facts behind why the parties are making the agreement. The recitals for a reciprocal landscaping easement agreement between Smith and Jones will follow the preamble that names and identifies the parties. The recitals might read as follows:

RECITALS

A. Smith[1] owns property in Multnomah County, Oregon legally described as Lot 7, Block 4, ASPHALT HEIGHTS (as so described, the "Smith Tract").

---

[1] I ordinarily use "Grantor," "Grantee," "Grantor Tract," and "Grantee Tract" to identify the parties and their property. In a reciprocal easement both parties are grantors and grantees, and I refer to them by name, or sometimes as "North Owner" and "South Owner" if their properties lay out that way. The tracts are then the "North Tract" and the "South Tract" and the reciprocal easement areas might be the "North Easement Area" and the "South Easement Area."

B. Jones owns property in Multnomah County, Oregon legally described as Lot 8, Block 4, ASPHALT HEIGHTS (as so described, the "Jones Tract"). The Jones Tract is adjacent to and south of the Smith Tract.

C. A fence installed by Smith's [or "Jones's," if appropriate] predecessors in interest some years ago near the property line common to the Smith Tract and the Jones Tract was recently surveyed and found to be south of the actual property line by a distance of about 18 inches at the west end and north of the actual property line by a distance of about 12 inches at the east end.

D. Smith and Jones wish to grant to each other reciprocal easements to maintain the fence in its current location [as long as it remains standing],[2] and to landscape the portion of each party's tract that is on the other party's side of the fence [while the fence is standing].[3]

With the recitals complete, you are ready to move on to the granting clauses of your easement agreement. If the parties are granting each other easements that are fully reciprocal, then the first four operative sections of your agreement might read as follows:

NOW, THEREFORE, SMITH AND JONES AGREE:

1. The recitals above are true and correct and are part of this Agreement.
2. Smith grants to Jones an easement to landscape and maintain the portion of the Smith Tract that lies south of the fence depicted on the attached Exhibit A[4] [and

[2] Before they sign the agreement, Smith and Jones should discuss what they will do when the time comes to replace the fence. Will they rebuild it in its current encroaching alignment, or will they rebuild it, if at all, on the true property line? The bracketed language in Recital D assumes that they would rebuild the fence on the actual property line.

[3] As with the previous bracketed language in Recital D, include this bracketed language if Smith and Jones have agreed that any new fence will be on the true property line.

[4] You will have a map or sketch attached as Exhibit A to show the approximate (if you or the parties prepared it) or exact (if a surveyor prepared it) location of the Smith and Jones tracts, the boundary line, and the fence. If a surveyor prepares the

legally described on the attached Exhibit B],[5] hereinafter the "Jones Easement Area." The Jones Easement Area is approximately 12 inches wide at its east end, narrowing westward to a point where the existing fence crosses the property line between the Smith Tract and the Jones Tract.

3. Jones grants to Smith an easement to landscape and maintain the portion of the Jones Tract that lies north of the fence depicted on the attached Exhibit A [and legally described on the attached Exhibit C],[6] hereinafter the "Smith Easement Area." The Smith Easement Area is approximately 18 inches wide at its west end, narrowing eastward to a point where the existing fence crosses the property line between the Smith Tract and the Jones Tract.
4. Smith and Jones each grant to the other an easement to maintain, repair, and when necessary replace the fence that lies between the Smith Tract and the Jones Tract. Any replacement of the fence will be [in the same location as the existing fence] [on the true property line, at which time this Agreement and the easements created hereunder will terminate].[7]

Note that I've distinguished between the Smith Tract (the entire parcel that Smith owns) and the Jones Easement Area (the portion of the Smith Tract that Jones gets to landscape). I include the legal description of the Smith Tract and the Jones Tract because I want title company indexers to put the recorded easement agreement in the proper lot book in their title plants. I separately described the Smith Easement Area and the Jones Easement Area to make it clear that the easement agreement does not encumber their entire parcels, but only the described portions. Many older easement

---

map, ask the surveyor to show the nearest corners and walls of the houses on the Smith and Jones tracts.

[5] Include the bracketed language if a surveyor has provided you with a legal description of the Jones Easement Area.

[6] Include the bracketed language if a surveyor has provided you with a legal description of the Smith Easement Area.

[7] Again, the parties should agree on whether a replacement fence will be in the same location or on the true property line. I'll discuss this point further in section 9.3.

agreements, and (alas) some modern agreements, describe the parties' tracts but don't clearly state that only a specific portion of the tracts are subject to the easement. When one owner wants to redevelop, a cautious lender will hesitate to lend on a new building if the lender can't be assured that the building won't encroach into the easement area.

9.2 Easements for Encroaching Buildings

Sometimes the encroachment problem is more serious than a fence and a few azaleas. Imagine that the surveyor discovered not only that the fence is not on the property line, but that a corner of the Smith house extends onto the Jones tract. The parties now want you to prepare an easement to legitimize the encroachment of the Smith house onto the Jones tract.

Again, begin by writing the recitals to describe the encroachment and why the parties are signing the agreement. Here is an example of a recital to describe an encroaching structure:

> C. A garage on the Grantee Tract encroaches by less than one foot onto the Grantor Tract. Grantor wishes to grant to Grantee a nonexclusive easement to maintain the garage in its current location as long as it remains standing.[8]

This recital identifies the encroaching structure (in this instance, an outbuilding) and the approximate extent of the encroachment (less than one foot). People who read this agreement ten years from now will be able to look at the property and figure out what the grantor and grantee intended the agreement to cover, especially if you attach a survey or sketch that shows the location of the encroachment in relation to the property line and other improvements.[9]

---

[8] The garage was some distance from the house. In this instance, the parties agreed that if the garage were torn down or destroyed, the garage owner would rebuild, if at all, only on the garage owner's own property.

[9] See section 4.7: when you are identifying where an encroachment is located, a word is worth one thousandth of a picture.

If the building encroaches by a few feet and you write an easement to keep the building in place that is limited to the building's footprint, how will the owner maintain the outside of the building? Illinois answered this question for single-family homes in 1998 when it adopted the "Entry on Adjoining Land To Accomplish Repairs Act."[10] The Repairs Act[11] states that if the owner of a single-family home that existed when the act became law needs access over a neighbor's property to maintain the house, the neighbor must allow access. The Repairs Act grants a cause of action against a neighbor who refuses to allow access. The Repairs Act does not apply only to houses that encroach on neighboring property, but to all houses in Illinois that were standing in 1998, and as far as I can tell it's unique to Illinois.

If you are writing an easement agreement for an encroaching house that is not in Illinois, then consider whether to include an access easement for a strip of land near the building, perhaps five feet wide, to allow the building owner to maintain and repair the building. If you draft the easement agreement to cover only the area that the building itself occupies, then the owner of the building can't patch, paint, and repair the building from the outside—the easement to keep the building in place does not automatically carry with it a right to enter the rest of the burdened property to maintain the building. Here is how you can provide a limited right of access for maintenance:

> XX. In addition to the right to maintain [and repair] [, repair, and replace][12] the portion of the improvement within the Easement Area, Grantor grants to Grantee a limited and nonexclusive right of access to the portion of the Grantor Tract that lies within 5.00 feet of the Easement Area for the sole purpose of [maintaining and repairing] [maintaining, repairing, and replacing] the improvement within the Easement Area. Grantee may

---

10 765 ILCS § 125.

11 I decline to shorten its name to the clunky acronym "EOALTARA."

12 Whether you choose "maintain and repair" or "maintain, repair, and replace" will depend on whether the grantor will allow the grantee to rebuild the improvement in the same location, or whether the easement will terminate if the encroaching improvement is destroyed.

> exercise this right only at reasonable times and after giving Grantor ___ days' notice of the proposed time, place, and purpose for Grantee's entry. Grantee will repair all damage to the Grantor Tract caused by Grantee's entry.

9.3 Demolition and Rebuilding

If you are writing an easement agreement to legitimize a fence or a building that encroaches on neighboring property, you should state what happens to the easement if the fence or building is demolished or destroyed. May the easement holder (the owner of the improvement) rebuild the fence or building in the same encroaching location, or must the easement holder rebuild on the holder's own property? Put more simply, when the encroachment no longer exists, will the easement continue or terminate?

In general, the grantor will want the easement to terminate if the encroachment is destroyed, and the grantee will want to be able to rebuild in the same location. Whatever their eventual agreement may be, you must state it in the easement agreement.

Here is language you can use if the easement for an encroaching fence will terminate if the fence is destroyed:

> XV. The easement described in this Agreement will terminate if the fence that is the subject of this Agreement is destroyed, demolished, or becomes so damaged or dilapidated that it is not reasonably possible to repair it. In that event [Grantor] [Grantee] [Grantor and Grantee jointly] will remove the fence and dispose of the fencing material, and Grantee's right to use the Easement Area will terminate. Either party may then record a notice of termination of the Agreement. Any replacement fence must thereafter be entirely on the property of the party who builds the fence, without encroaching onto the property of the other party.

If the encroaching neighbor has built improvements in reliance on the fence's location, as for example a tennis court, barbecue area, or walkways, then the parties may agree that a replacement fence can be in the same location. In that case, you might include this paragraph in the easement agreement:

> XV. The easement described in this Agreement will not terminate if the fence that is the subject of this Agreement is damaged or destroyed. In that event Grantee will replace the fence with [a similar fence of good quality] [another six-foot high sight-obscuring fence [of the same material [or other material acceptable to Grantor in Grantor's sole discretion]]][13] [at the sole expense of Grantee] [at the expense of Grantee, for which Grantor will reimburse one-half the cost].

[13] If the handsome cedar fence blows down and is destroyed, the grantor may be willing to let the grantee replace the fence in the same location with another cedar fence, but not with a cyclone or chicken-mesh fence. The time to negotiate the nature and appearance of the replacement fence is before the fence needs to be replaced.

10
Relocation Rights and Wrongs

A well-drafted easement agreement will exactly define the easement area and will include a map or site plan that matches the legal description of the easement area. Neither party may unilaterally relocate the easement without the consent of the other party unless the easement agreement allows one party to relocate the easement. When the parties have signed and recorded the easement agreement, the question of where the easement is located has been settled.

Or has it? Spurred by the Restatement (Third) of Property (2000), the trend is slowly growing to allow the servient owner to relocate an access easement without the consent of the dominant owner, under certain conditions. This chapter will discuss the Restatement's position and what the careful drafter might do to anticipate a change in the law.

10.1 The Restatement (Third) of Property

The Restatement (Third) of Property includes the following statement in Servitudes, § 4.8(3):

> Unless expressly denied by the terms of an easement, as defined in § 1.2, the owner of the servient estate is entitled to make reasonable changes in the location or dimensions of an easement,

at the servient owner's expense, to permit normal use or development of the servient estate, but only if the changes do not

(a) significantly lessen the utility of the easement,
(b) increase the burdens on the owner of the easement in its use and enjoyment, or
(c) frustrate the purpose for which the easement was created.

This section of the Restatement was not a statement of the common law of easements as it existed in 2000, but was the editors' proposal of what they would like the law to be. Only two states, Kentucky and Louisiana, had permitted the owner of the burdened property to unilaterally relocate an easement. Restatements are persuasive, however, and by 2017 the courts of at least six more states had expressly adopted the Restatement's position as the law.[1]

However, in 2020, the National Conference of Commissioners on Uniform State Laws (NCCUSL) issued a model act, entitled the Uniform Easement Relocation Act, that would prohibit the grantor from waiving its right to relocate the easement area:

4(b) The right under subsection (a) to relocate an easement may not be waived, excluded, or restricted by agreement even if:

(1) the instrument creating the easement contains language requiring consent of the parties to amend the terms of the easement; or
(2) the location of the easement is fixed by the instrument creating the easement, another agreement, previous conduct, acquiescence, estoppel, or implication.[2]

---

[1] The states are Colorado, Massachusetts, Nebraska, New York, South Dakota, and Vermont. Much of the information comes from a March 13, 2018 memorandum that Professor John A. Lovett of Loyola University New Orleans College of Law presented to the Drafting Committee of the Relocation of Non-Utility Easements Act, based on John A. Lovett, Diane B. Davies, & James C. Smith, *A Deep Dive into Easements*, THE ACREL PAPERS, Fall 2017, at 23–108, https://www.uniformlaws.org/viewdocument/reporters-memo-to-drafting-committ?CommunityKey=3cf8b521-0859-4483-925c-aa0edca3a541&tab=librarydocuments (retrieved February 14, 2020).

[2] https://www.uniformlaws.org/HigherLogic/System/DownloadDocumentFile.ashx?DocumentFileKey=e698152e-005c-b271-d0ef-19257b5e9435&forceDialog=0 (retrieved February 15, 2020).

As of this writing (spring 2021), the Act has been enacted in Nebraska, and has been introduced into the 2021 sessions of the legislatures of Colorado, West Virginia, Utah, and Nevada. The prudent drafter who represents the dominant estate should consider the possibility that more states will adopt the Act, possibly with revisions specific to the adopting states.

10.2 Drafting around the Restatement and the Uniform Easement Relocation Act

The first part of § 4.8(3) of the Restatement, "Unless expressly denied by the terms of an easement," contemplates that the parties to an easement agreement may opt out of the relocation provision; that is, they may include in their easement agreement a provision that prohibits the owner of the servient property from exercising the right to relocate the easement. The parties can include this language in an easement agreement to opt out of the Restatement's position:

> IX. Notwithstanding any statutory or common-law right that Grantor may have to relocate the Easement Area, Grantor and Grantee agree that Grantor shall have no right to relocate the Easement Area without the consent of Grantee, which Grantee may withhold in Grantee's sole discretion.

The parties can opt out of the Restatement rule, but they cannot opt out of the Uniform Easement Relocation Act if the state where the property is located adopts it. If the exact location of the easement area is important to the grantee, then consider including in the easement agreement a specific description about what in the easement is important to the grantee. You could include this clause, for which I've given some examples of facts that might be important to the purchaser of an access easement. The language in Section XI is taken directly from Section 4 of the Uniform Easement Relocation Act:

> X. If, notwithstanding Section IX of this Agreement, the State of ____ adopts the Uniform Easement Relocation Act or any other statute that makes Grantor's waiver in Section IX void or unenforceable, then the parties agree that the following

characteristics of the Easement Area are essential to their bargain and to Grantee's use of the Easement Area:

i. The traveled portion of the Easement Area is not less than ___ feet wide throughout;
ii. A clear area not less than ___ feet wide will exist and be maintained on each side of the traveled portion to allow for overhanging vehicles;
iii. No curve on the Easement Area has a radius of less than ___ feet measured at the centerline;
iv. No part of the traveled portion of the Easement Area will have a grade of more than ____ percent; and
v. The Easement Area enters the Grantee Tract at the point shown on Exhibit ___ at an angle of no more than ___ degrees from the perpendicular to the property line.

XI. Grantor and Grantee agree that any proposed relocation of the Easement Area that does not satisfy each of the characteristics listed in Section X will materially lessen the utility of the easement for Grantee, will increase the burden on Grantee in its reasonable use and enjoyment of the easement, and will frustrate the affirmative, easement-related purposes for which the easement was created.

10.3 Can the Dominant Owner Relocate the Easement?

At common law, the owner of the dominant estate (the easement holder) did not have the right to relocate the easement across the servient estate unless the easement agreement gave the easement holder the right to relocate the easement. If you hold an easement to build and use a driveway on a specified path across your neighbor's property, you can't relocate the driveway to some other part of your neighbor's property that's more convenient to you, even if the relocation wouldn't affect your neighbor.

The Uniform Easement Relocation Act does not change the common-law rule, which its drafters noted in Comment 3 to Section 4 of the Model Act. The drafters of the Act did describe an Illinois court as holding that the court's decision to allow the owner of property subject to a driveway easement to relocate the easement, which the court found to be consistent with Section 4.8(3) of the Restatement (Third) of Property, was also consistent with Illinois precedent "allowing either the dominant or servient estate owner to make changes to an easement as long as the changes are not 'substantial."[3] The Illinois appellate opinion that the drafters cited, *McGoey v. Brace*, in turn cited two earlier Illinois decisions in which the dominant owner (the easement holder) unilaterally changed the nature of the easement. In one case the easement holder replaced a dilapidated bridge to an island in a lake with an asphalt causeway, which the court held unreasonably interfered with the rights of the lake owner.[4] In the other case, the holder of an easement to maintain a septic drainfield on a neighbor's property changed the contours of the neighbor's land, which the court found to be a substantial alteration of the easement.[5] Although the courts in both cases recognized the possibility that an easement holder might unilaterally alter an easement if the alteration produced no substantial effect on the servient property, in neither case did the courts approve the alteration, and in neither case was the alteration a relocation.

Despite the suggestion in the comments to the Act that an easement holder may relocate an easement without the consent of the owner of the servient estate if the change is insubstantial, the common law is still strongly against giving the easement holder the right to relocate the easement. Nothing in the Act changes that principle—the relocation right belongs only to the servient owner, unless the easement agreement gives the easement holder a right to relocate the easement.

If you are drafting an easement agreement for the easement holder, your client does not expect to need to relocate the easement area in the future. Presumably your client negotiated to have an easement in the location that your client wants. You should, however, think about the possibility that if the law or building codes change, your client may want to relocate the easement, or change its burden on the servient property.

---

[3] Uniform Easement Relocation Act, Comment 3 to Section 4, citing McGoey v. Brace, 918 N.E. 2d 559, 563-67 (Ill. App. Ct. 2009).

[4] Triplett v. Beuckman, 40 Ill. App.3d 379 (1976).

[5] Professional Executive Center v. LaSalle National Bank, 211 Ill. App.3d 368 (1991).

For example, suppose that your client is buying a private utility easement to install poles and string wires across the neighbor's property to provide power to the client's house. The easement allows your client, perhaps, to install four poles up to fifteen feet high, in specified locations, so that the wires will be at least twelve feet from the ground, the current code requirement.[6] Your client installs the poles and wires. A few years later, the government changes the electrical code and the wires must now be fifteen feet above the ground, or perhaps the code now requires five poles to span the distance, or perhaps a road-widening project takes out one of the poles, which cannot be replaced in the permitted location. Your client needs to move the line, or put an additional or replacement pole in a different location. What should your client do?[7]

You can include language in your easement agreement to cover this situation. If the easement is for utility lines, you could use this language as a starting point:

> **X. Alteration and relocation to comply with law.** If a government with jurisdiction adopts a law, code, or regulation affecting Grantee's use of or improvements in the Easement Area that requires Grantee to change or relocate Grantee's improvements in the Easement Area, then the Easement Area and its allowable use by Grantee will be automatically extended or expanded by the minimum amount necessary to allow Grantee to construct improvements that comply with the law, code, or regulation and that are sufficient for Grantee to continue to receive the benefits of this Agreement.

You should be cautious about using that language for a driveway easement unless you have considered how it will mesh with the paragraph that states the permitted use. What happens if your easement agreement authorizes the holder to construct and use a driveway

[6] This book is not a treatise on the National Electrical Code and may not be cited as authority in any dispute over clearances. Nor should you use it as guidance on safety measures for your home electrical work.

[7] Other than grovel at the feet of the neighbor, which can be an effective tactic but is not usually one's first choice.

"for residential purposes" without imposing a limit on the number of dwelling units that can use the driveway.[8] Perhaps your local code requires the driveway that serves a single house to be twelve feet wide, and the grantor grants an easement for a fifteen-foot-wide strip within which the grantee may build a driveway twelve feet wide. Everything is fine until the easement holder converts the house on the benefited property into a fourplex. Local code requires the driveway to a four-unit building to be at least eighteen feet wide. If you did not adequately limit the easement holder to using the driveway for one unit only, and if you have plain-vanilla language to allow the grantee to expand or relocate the easement, then when the grantee decides to build the fourplex and demands to widen the driveway to be eighteen feet wide "to comply with the code," the grantor will have an expensive fight.

10.4 A Special Kind of Relocation: Relocation by Adverse Possession

I encountered one unusual situation where a property developer wished to use an old access easement as one of two access points to its subdivision. The access easement had been written fifty years earlier to provide access across three tracts to a fourth tract. The three tracts were only an acre or two in size; the fourth tract was many acres. The easement was thirty feet wide, with a shared driveway about fifteen feet wide. City code allowed the developer to count the easement as an access point only if it was at least twenty-four feet wide. The first tract bordered a public street; the second and third tracts did not border a street and relied on the easement for access.

The developer bought the second, third, and fourth tracts and announced plans for the subdivision. The owner of the first tract then sued, alleging that over many years she had planted landscaping, including trees that were quite large at the time of the suit, up to the edge of the traveled driveway and had therefore extinguished the

[8] See section 4.4 about limiting the purposes for which the grantee can use the easement area.

easement over the landscaped area by adverse possession.[9] With the landscaped area excluded, the remaining easement area was less than twenty-four feet wide, not wide enough for the developer to count it as a required access point to the subdivision.

If your client is acquiring an easement for development in the distant future that is wider than what your client needs right now—for example, a forty-foot-wide easement for a driveway that won't be wider than fifteen feet until the time comes to develop the property, you can draft around this situation by imposing an obligation on the owners of the easement area to reconfirm the easement upon the request of an easement holder. Here is one possible clause to include in your easement agreement:

> XX. Until the Grantee requires or wishes the use of the entire Easement Area for access to the Grantee Tract, Grantor may plant trees and shrubs and make minor improvements in the portion of the Easement Area that is not actually used for the access road, and may fence that portion as Grantor wishes. Grantor agrees that Grantee may remove any fence, trees, shrubs, and minor improvements when Grantee wishes to use that portion of the Easement Area for access, it being agreed by Grantor and Grantee that Grantor's continued use of the non-traveled portions of the Easement Area is permissive and not adverse to the rights of Grantee.

[9] A professor of property law who reads this far will explain that the owner of the first tract can't acquire title to the easement area by adverse possession because she already has fee title. Regardless of the technical term, her claim was essentially one of adverse possession: for more than ten years (the statutory period in Oregon), she had actively planted and maintained trees and landscaping in a portion of the easement area to the exclusion of the other people who had the right to use the easement area for access.

11
Ten Ways to Misdraft Your Easement Agreement

You have read ten chapters of my advice on how to draft an easement agreement. This chapter provides equal time for the opposition. Here are ten ways that you can misdraft an easement agreement, cause confusion for your client, and give rise to litigation.

11.1 First Error: Don't Define Your Terms, and Don't Use the Terms You Have Defined

It is a convention of legal drafting that a capitalized word in an agreement that is not ordinarily capitalized has a special meaning, which the agreement must then define. Some agreements define terms when they first appear, as in this preamble to an easement agreement that is entitled "Easement Agreement":

> This Easement Agreement (this "Agreement") is made by Morrison Horner ("Grantor"), as grantor, and James Holmes and Mary Holmes (together, "Grantees"), as grantees.

Long agreements will often collect most or all defined terms into one section near the beginning or the end, entitled "Defined Terms" or "Definitions," and will include a clause near the beginning that states "Capitalized terms not otherwise defined in this Agreement have the meanings given to them in Section ___."

I often see old agreements, and sometimes I see not-so-old agreements, that use terms like "Property" and "Premises" without defining what the words mean. Do they refer to the same tract? To different tracts? It is a guess.

I like to begin drafting an agreement by listing the terms that I will want to define and then use. For an easement agreement, these will always include Grantor, Grantee, Grantor Tract, Grantee Tract, and Easement Area. If I'm writing an easement agreement for a driveway and utility lines that already exist, I may also define Driveway Area and Utility Lines to be the existing facilities. If I'm writing an easement between two existing buildings, I may also define the buildings as the Grantor Building and the Grantee Building.

Once I've defined the terms, I use them. When I've defined "Grantor Tract" I will call the grantor's property the Grantor Tract throughout. If I were to refer to the Grantor Tract as "the real estate owned by Grantor," then a court might infer that, because I'd defined "Grantor Tract," the term "the real estate owned by Grantor" must mean something different from "Grantor Tract," even though that wasn't what I had intended.

11.2 Second Error: Don't Identify the Benefited Property

I routinely define the grantor's property as the "Grantor Tract" and the grantee's property as the "Grantee Tract" and include a legal description of each as an exhibit to the easement agreement.

You may have encountered, as I have, old easement agreements in which the grantor is stated to own certain property and is granting an access easement across the grantor's property to the grantee "for access to the adjacent lands owned by the grantee." Ninety years later, the reader knows where the easement is, but not what land it benefits, at least not without extensively researching old land records to figure out what adjacent land the grantee owned in 1930. Don't create problems for the real estate lawyers of 2110 by not describing and defining what property the easement benefits.

11.3 Third Error: Don't Identify the Actual Servient Property

This drafting error should be rare, but it isn't. It comes in three different flavors.

First, as is usually the case, when the area subject to the easement is only a portion of the grantor's parcel, the drafter should distinguish between the easement area and the rest of the parcel. If the drafter does not carefully distinguish the easement area from the rest of the parcel, then the easement agreement when recorded will create an encumbrance on the entire parcel that will impede later development.

If you use one defined term for the grantor's parcel and a second defined term for the easement area itself, then you will avoid this mistake. For example, in a reciprocal easement to document a shared driveway that uses parts of both properties, you might include recitals like these:

A. Grantee owns certain real property in Multnomah County, Oregon legally described in **Exhibit A** (the "**Grantee Tract**").

B. Grantor owns certain real property in Multnomah County, Oregon legally described in **Exhibit B** (the **"Grantor Tract"**). The Grantor Tract is partially adjacent to and generally west of the Grantee Tract.

C. For many years Grantee has had a gravel driveway (the **"Driveway"**) generally following the westernmost property line of the Grantee Tract from the southern property line to the house located on the Grantee Tract. A small portion of the Driveway encroaches on the Grantor Tract.

D. The parties desire to grant reciprocal easements allowing for Grantee to continue to use that portion of the Grantor Tract shown on the attached **Exhibit C** as the **"Easement Area"** as a gravel driveway, and allowing for Grantee to use that portion of the Driveway shown on the attached **Exhibit C** as the **"Shared Driveway Area"** for the purpose of ingress and egress to and from the Grantee Tract.

Then the granting clause will read as follows:

1. Grantor hereby grants to Grantee the nonexclusive right to use the Easement Area for the purpose only of vehicular and pedestrian access to and from the Grantee Tract.

Note that the grant is limited to rights in the Easement Area, which is shown on an attached map. The grant does not cover the entire Grantor Tract.

Also note that the recitals identify both the Grantor Tract and the Grantee Tract by legal description. A drafter who does not take the time to obtain both legal descriptions might come up with the following:

A. Grantee owns certain real property in Multnomah County, Oregon legally described in **Exhibit A** (the "**Grantee Tract**").
B. Grantor owns real property in Multnomah County, Oregon (the **"Grantor Tract"**) that is adjacent to the Grantee Tract.

What's missing? This is the error I described in section 11.2, except that the parties are reversed. The easement agreement identifies only one property and describes the other one by its relative location, and not by an actual legal description.

One of your goals in writing an easement agreement is to make it as easy as possible for your local title companies to index the recorded easement agreement against the Grantor Tract—that is, to place a copy of the easement agreement into the lot book (or its electronic equivalent) that includes the Grantor Tract, so that a future insurer of the title to the Grantor Tract will find the easement agreement and include it as an exception to title in its title reports, its title policies, and on deeds to the Grantor Tract. You want your county's title insurers to notify future owners of the Grantor Tract that the easement agreement restricts the Grantor Tract. Make it easy for them to find your agreement.

11.4 Fourth Error: Don't Describe the Extent and Intensity of the Use

Which error to commit here depends on which party you represent. If you represent the servient owner, you should write the easement to strictly limit the use that the dominant owner can make of the easement area. You can do your client a disservice if you don't limit how much use the dominant owner can make of the easement area.

11.4.1 Don't Protect the Burdened Owner by Limiting the Easement Holder

To repeat an example from chapter 4, if your client gives an easement to the adjoining owner "for ingress, egress, and utility service" that is not limited by type of use (e.g., "for one single-family residence") and a later owner develops the neighboring property with a shopping center, using the easement area as one of the access points, your client will blame you for the flood of traffic, especially on the day after Thanksgiving. Your client did not set a price on the access easement to make up for the noise and bustle of holiday shopping traffic.

Your client has one chance to limit how the easement holder will use the easement area. If you miss that chance when you're drafting the easement agreement, your client will never have that chance again.

11.4.2 Don't Protect the Easement Holder by Allowing the Intensity of the Use to Increase as the Easement Holder's Needs Change

Conversely, if you represent the party that is buying the easement, you will want to make sure that the easement agreement does not unreasonably restrict what your client can do with the property in the future. Even if your client doesn't plan to build a shopping center, you should consider how the use of the property is likely to change in the future, and whether those changes are reasonably foreseeable.

Consider our basic access easement, in which Tract Two obtains an access easement across Tract One. The owner of Tract One asks to limit the easement to serve "one single-family dwelling unit." Perhaps Tract Two is large enough for the owner to some day build a guest cottage. Perhaps the house is large enough for the owner to build an accessory dwelling unit inside the house.[1] If the easement allows

[1] The term is slowly replacing the older term "mother-in-law apartment" and the even older term "granny flat."

use for residential purposes only, then it may not allow the easement holder to use the accessway for a business that the holder conducts from the house, what land use codes sometimes call a "home occupation" or a "cottage industry." Think not just about what your client *is* doing at the property, but also about what your client *could* be doing at the property.

11.5 Fifth Error: Don't Describe the Allowed Use in Exact Language

If you are drafting an easement agreement that grants the adjoining owner the right to build a driveway and install power and phone lines, and specifies how wide the driveway may be and how high (or low) the lines may be, you don't need to worry too much about how you describe the use. If the rights you are granting are more complicated, not just the rights to install utility lines and cross the Grantor Tract on a specified path but to use portions of the Grantor Tract for longer periods of time, then you should be as exact as you can.

Here's an example from Michigan of what can happen when easement drafters use mushy or undefined words. The defendant owned four adjacent lots, which from west to east were numbered 782, 781, 780, and 772. Lots 782 and 772 fronted on a lake; Lots 781 and 780 were north of Lot 782, west of Lot 772, and had no lake frontage. The defendant lived in a house on Lot 772. The defendant and her then-husband sold Lots 781 and 782 and reserved an easement over the east twenty feet of those lots for the benefit of Lots 780 and 772, using this clause:

> The Grantors reserve an easement over the East 20 feet of Lots 781 and 782 of Lake Ogemaw No. 7 Subdivision for ingress and egress to Lake Ogemaw and for the personal use and occupation by the owners of Lots 772 and 780 of Lake Ogemaw No. 7 Subdivision.

The east twenty feet of Lots 781 and 782 ran from the southeast corner of Lot 780 (a non-lakefront lot) and along the entire west line of Lot 772 (which had other lake frontage), south to the lake.

This clause appears to reserve two or three rights for the benefit of Lots 780 and 772: (a) the right to use the easement area for ingress and egress to Lake Ogemaw, and (b) the right to the "personal use and occupation" of the easement area. It's possible that "personal use" and "occupation" are two different rights, which would make the number of easement rights three in total.

Three years after reserving the easement for Lots 772 and 780, the defendant extinguished the easement rights of Lot 772, which had its own lake frontage, and sold Lot 772. She built a house on Lot 780 (not lakefront) and moved into it.

The defendant used the easement area to moor her boat and store her personal property. She built a fire pit in the easement area. The owners of Lot 772 sued her for exceeding the scope of the easement. The owners of Lots 781 and 782 were later joined to the suit.

At trial and on appeal the question was, what did the defendant mean when she reserved the right to "personal use and occupation" of the easement area? The parties presented evidence about how the defendant was actually using the easement area. The defendant testified that when she reserved the easement, she believed that she could do "anything" in the easement area. The appellate court ruled that the word "occupation" was inherently ambiguous in the context of an easement, because (citing an earlier Michigan case) "an easement does not displace the general possession of the land by its owner, but merely grants the holder of the easement *qualified* possession only to the extent necessary for enjoyment of the rights conferred by the easement."[2]

Because the word "occupation" was ambiguous, the court reviewed the evidence of how the defendant actually used the easement area. The trial court held, and the appellate court affirmed, that she could use the easement area to moor a boat in season, and that she could sunbathe and picnic, but that she had to remove her belongings other than the boat when she had finished for the day. She could not build a firepit or any other permanent structure.[3]

If the defendant had wanted to reserve the right to build a firepit or other permanent recreational improvements in the easement area,

---

2 Schadewald v. Brule, 225 Mich. App. 26, 35 (1997) (emphasis added by court).

3 Steenland v. Tousciuk, No. 341084 (Mich. App. 2019, unpublished).

she should have said so. Would the parties have gone to trial and the court of appeals if her lawyer had written the reservation clause more clearly, for example, like this?

> The Grantors reserve an easement over the East 20 feet of Lots 781 and 782 of Lake Ogemaw No. 7 Subdivision for the benefit of Lots 772 and 780 of Lake Ogemaw No. 7 Subdivision, for the following purposes:
>
> (a) Ingress and egress to and from Lake Ogemaw;
> (b) The mooring of boats and personal watercraft for their recreational use;
> (c) Recreational use such as picnicking, sunbathing, and other outdoor recreation; and
> (d) Storage and use of recreational personal property such as chairs, picnic tables, and outdoor grills; and
> (e) Construction and use of unenclosed recreational improvements such as firepits, horseshoe courts, and the like.

It's an easy error to think that because you don't know any detail about what your client wants to do in the easement area, you will use language that is as vague as possible, such as "personal use and occupation." You and your client run the risk that a court will find the words you choose to be as vague as you do. Don't make a court describe your client's easement rights for you. Take the time to find and write the right words.

11.6 Sixth Error: Don't Set Standards for Roads and Utilities

If you are advising the servient owner through whose property the road and utility lines will pass, then you should insist that the easement agreement state what improvements the dominant owner can build in the easement area, and how large they can be. A grantor may be willing to convey a thirty-foot-wide easement for access and utilities without expecting that the grantee will build a thirty-foot-wide road instead of a twelve-foot-wide driveway.

Similarly, a grantor may be willing to allow the grantee to install overhead power and telephone lines on conventional wooden poles to serve one or two houses without being willing to accept higher-voltage lines to serve a subdivision. If your easement agreement allows the grantee to install utility lines to serve the Grantee Tract and a few years later the owner proposes to build forty houses on the Grantee Tract, your client may ask you why the easement agreement you drafted doesn't prohibit the neighbor from running the subdivision's tall power lines through the easement area.

11.7 Seventh Error: Don't Attach a Map of the Properties and the Easement Area

You can write the best easement agreement in the nation, and attach the finest legal descriptions from a top-notch surveyor, and yet your client and the other party will understand the agreement much better if you also attach a map of the properties and the easement area. Even a simple map that shows the easement area in relation to the property lines and the nearest road will make it easier for future readers to identify your easement. Insisting on a map serves another purpose: it gives your client one more chance to verify that the easement is where your client intends it to be. If you have a surveyor draft the legal description of the easement area, then the surveyor will also be able to provide a plot that shows the easement area in relation to the property lines and possibly the existing improvements. The map is the final safety measure to assure that the grantor and grantee have truly agreed on where the easement area is to be.

You may believe that you can get by without a map if the Grantor Tract is Lot 7 and the Grantee Tract is Lot 8 of the same subdivision, and if the easement area is as simple as "the west ten feet of Lot 7." And you may. But consider: is Lot 7 a rectangle, with a straight line as its west boundary? If the west boundary is curved, or if it consists of several straight lines that run in slightly different directions, maybe "the west ten feet of Lot 7" has several different possible meanings. And if Lot 7 is a rectangle that is not oriented to the points of the compass, which of its two westerly boundary lines does "the west ten feet of Lot 7" refer to? Be safe: include a map.

11.8 Eighth Error: Don't Deal With Development and Relocation for the Grantor

Your client and the other party may expect the area to remain unchanged for decades to come. Your client may tell you, "Why should we worry about future development when nothing is going to happen for our lifetimes?" When I was born, the city I live in and the two nearest suburbs were quiet country towns that had a combined population of 14,000 people. Today the three cities hold 125,000 people. Dirt roads have been graveled, graveled roads have been paved, and paved roads have been widened. Yesterday's farm is today's subdivision or shopping center. Today's country estate may be tomorrow's subdivision or shopping center.

If you represent the grantor of a small easement through a large tract in the path of development, you can reserve for the grantor the right to relocate the easement if the grantor should want to move the easement when the property is developed. The grantee may not care if the grantor relocates a utility line easement—electricity will flow to the grantee regardless of the easement's route—but the grantor's grandchildren will be unhappy if the grantee's grandchildren can use an immovable easement to hamstring the project.

11.9 Ninth Error: Don't Deal With Relocation for the Grantee

The ninth error is the flip side of the eighth error: whether and how you deal with the relocation question when you represent the grantee. As I discussed in chapter 10, the Restatement (Third) of Property has taken the position that the owner of the servient property should be able, in some circumstances, to relocate an access or utility easement without the consent of the dominant owner. The Uniform Easement Relocation Act, a project of the Uniform Law Commission, would prohibit parties to an easement from waiving the right of the servient owner to relocate an easement. Even if relocating an easement is not yet an issue in your state, it is likely to become an issue sometime in the next five to ten years. If you represent the grantee and you don't include in the easement agreement a statement of the factors that are most important to your client, you and your client take the chance that your state adopts the Restatement's position or enacts the Uniform Easement Relocation Act, and then a judge will decide what factors were in your client's mind when your client acquired the easement. For a short driveway across one property to get to another, relocation may not be an issue. For a longer accessway, or an accessway intended for future development, the question whether the servient owner can relocate the easement, and if so to where, may become essential to your client. Why not draft a response to the law in advance?

11.10 Tenth Error: Don't Ask How Your Client Is Going to Use the Benefited Property

The tenth way that you can misdraft an easement is actually a counseling error rather than a drafting error. Your client is partitioning a tract of land, intending to sell the front half and keep the back half. Only the front half borders a public street. Your client wants you to draw up an easement agreement or a declaration of easement so that the client will retain access across the front half to get to and from the back half.

You could go to your form bank, select an easement agreement for an accessway, change the names of the parties and the legal descriptions, and provide it to your client. Your client will have exactly what your client asked you to draft: an easement across the front half that provides your client with access to the back half. Instead of giving your client only what your client described, ask what your client will do with the back half, and think about what your client might need.

For example, if your client is going to build one house on the back half, your client will use the easement area for a driveway. How wide does local code require a driveway to be? If you pulled a form that you used for a twelve-foot-wide driveway and local code requires a driveway to a single house to be fifteen feet wide, your easement will be technically correct and practically unusable.

If your client will build a house on the back half, the house will need to be connected to water, electric, phone, and cable lines, and possibly to natural gas and sanitary sewer lines as well. Does your chosen form allow your client to install utility lines in the easement area to connect the new house to lines in the public street? Clients in cold, candle-lit houses with no working toilets tend to be cranky.

Maybe your client is going to build a fourplex on the back half. How wide does local code require a driveway to be if it serves four units instead of one? In some jurisdictions a driveway must be wider if it serves more than a certain number of units. Your chosen form may allow a driveway wide enough to serve one house. Your client will be unhappy when the zoning people say that the driveway is not wide enough to serve a four-unit apartment.

Conclusion

We're almost done! Now that you and I are at the last chapter, I'd like to reiterate the most important principles I want to communicate through this book:

- Define and use your terms properly. Be consistent throughout your easement agreement.
- State in your easement agreement whether it's an easement in gross or appurtenant to particular property. If it's appurtenant, identify the property.
- Distinguish between the entire Grantor Tract and that portion which is the Easement Area. Don't inadvertently burden the entire Grantor Tract with an easement that's supposed to affect only a small part of the tract.
- Use maps and diagrams. A word is worth one millipicture.
- Make friends with surveyors. They know stuff.
- Think not only of the present but of the future. Your words are going to be a sort of private law between the parties and their successors for decades to come. Craft them carefully.

- Avoid the passive voice. If you are imposing an obligation on a party, write that the party will do something, not that something is to be done.
- If the grantor is granting several rights, list the rights with subheadings or in sections. Make your agreement as easy as possible for the future reader to understand.
- Make your easement agreement as easy as possible for your local title insurers to index correctly.

Appendix

Here are six easement agreements that you can use as starting points for drafting easement agreements for your clients. These are not off-the-shelf agreements; each has provisions that I drafted for the specific parties involved. I have replaced the names of the parties and the locations with names that the astute reader will recognize as being drawn from literature and history.

The Access Easement Agreement and the Easement Maintenance Agreement are two renditions of access easements and incorporate many of the ideas about access easements that chapter 5 covers. The Reciprocal Easement Agreement is a multiparty access agreement for an existing private road and bridge. It touches lightly on some of the encroachment topics that I discussed in chapter 9. It also shows one way to handle an agreement with many grantees.

The Utility Easement Agreement is an example of a utility easement appurtenant to the grantee's property (see chapter 6 on appurtenant utility easements). This agreement has the pleasing wrinkle of having two grantors who each owns one tract and one grantee who owns two separate tracts. I've included it as an example of an agreement with more than one grantor, as well as how to draft a utility agreement when the easement area is already in use as a private road.

The View Easement Agreement embodies many of the ideas that I covered in chapter 8. The grantee owned property with an unobstructed view of the ocean and went to great effort to define the protected view as exactly as possible so that prospective buyers of the downhill property would know the restrictions.

The Landscaping Easement Agreement demonstrates how two friendly adjoining landowners can agree to treat an established fence line as their common boundary for practical purposes without undertaking the expensive process of obtaining a property line adjustment.

I've included annotations to explain what I thought about as I drafted these agreements. Please use the agreements not as templates to cut and paste wholesale but as intelligent checklists of the issues that you should consider when you draft an easement agreement.

- Access Easement Agreement
- Easement Maintenance Agreement
- Reciprocal Easement Agreement
- Utility Easement Agreement
- View Easement Agreement
- Landscaping Easement Agreement

Access Easement Agreement

Grantor: HUDSON, Martha
HUDSON, John H.
47 Garrideb Road
Eastbourne, Oregon

Grantee: JONES, Athelney
4 Whitehall Place
Eastbourne, Oregon

Affects: [insert tax parcel numbers here]

After recording return to:
Dean N. Alterman
Alterman Law Group PC
805 SW Broadway, Suite 1580
Portland, Oregon 97205

ACCESS EASEMENT AGREEMENT

This ACCESS EASEMENT AGREEMENT (this "Agreement") is entered into as of March ____, 2020 by and between MARTHA HUDSON and JOHN H. HUDSON, together "Grantors," and ATHELNEY JONES, hereinafter "Grantee," in connection with property in Sussex County, Oregon owned by Grantors and an adjoining property owned by Grantee.

RECITALS

A. Grantors own a parcel of real property in Section 4, Township 1 North, Range 6 East of the Willamette Meridian, in Sussex County, Oregon, legally described in the attached **Exhibit A** (the "Grantor Tract"). The house on the Grantor Tract currently has an address of 47 Garrideb Road, Eastbourne, Oregon.

B. Grantee owns a parcel of vacant real property in Sussex County, Oregon, legally described on the attached **Exhibit B** (the "Grantee Tract"). The Grantee Tract is adjacent to and east of the Grantor Tract.

C. The Grantor Tract is accessible by Garrideb Road, a public road that ends at the west end of the Grantor Tract and does not continue eastward to the Grantee Tract. A private driveway runs eastward through the Grantor Tract from the end of Garrideb Road to a point near the boundary between the Grantor Tract and the Grantee Tract.

D. The Grantee Tract does not border a public or private road. Grantee wishes to obtain pedestrian and vehicle access to the Grantee Tract from Garrideb Road over the private driveway on the Grantor Tract, and to obtain the right to extend utility lines to the Grantee Tract along the course of the private driveway.

E. Grantors and Grantee wish to enter into this Agreement to allow Grantee to access the Grantee Tract over the private driveway on the Grantor Tract for residential, agricultural, and recreational purposes and to extend utility services to the Grantee Tract. Grantors and Grantee also wish to set out the terms and conditions that will govern Grantee's use of the private driveway for the benefit of the Grantee Tract, and to provide for the maintenance and repair of the private driveway.

NOW, THEREFORE, GRANTORS AND GRANTEE AGREE:

1. Grant of Easement. For good consideration, Grantors hereby grant to Grantee for the benefit of, and appurtenant to,[1] the Grantee Tract, a non-exclusive, perpetual easement for pedestrian and light vehicle ingress and egress between Garrideb Road and the Grantee Tract, over and across the private road (the "Easement Area") that is located in approximately the location depicted on the attached **Exhibit C**, and legally described on the attached **Exhibit D**. The easement is limited to the purpose of access for private recreational and agricultural use of the Grantee Tract, including the right to use the Easement Area for access to one and only one single-family dwelling unit on the Grantee Tract,[2] and does not include any right to extend the benefit of the easement to property other than the Grantee Tract.[3] The Grantee may, however, install utility lines within the Easement Area, outside the portion of the Easement Area that the driveway occupies, to serve the Grantee Tract, at the sole expense of the Grantee and in a manner that does not unreasonably interfere with Grantors' use of the Easement Area and the rest of the Grantor Tract.

2. AS IS. Grantee accepts the use of the Easement Area in its present condition, AS IS, with all defects, apparent or latent, without any representation or warranty by Grantors or any representative of Grantors, expressed or implied. Grantee hereby assumes all risk of Grantee's use of the Easement Area.

3. Maintenance and Repair Obligations. Neither Grantors nor Grantee shall have any duty or obligation to maintain, inspect, or repair the Easement Area to any extent

[1] If I'm creating an appurtenant easement, I like to use the word "appurtenant" in the easement agreement so as to leave no mistake about the parties' intention. For a common driveway that serves two houses in an urban area, where there is no nearby property to partition or develop, I would not be worried about the consequences of leaving the word out. I wrote this agreement for properties in a rural area, where it was possible that one or the other party would acquire land that adjoined the two relevant tracts and then want to extend the driveway to serve more land, and more houses, than just the one house on each parcel.

[2] The Grantors are limiting the Grantee's use of the easement and guarding against future development of the Grantee Tract in a way that would increase the traffic on the Grantors' driveway beyond what one house would create.

[3] Even though the grant of an easement does not include "pass-through" rights (see sections 4.3 and 4.4.5 of this book), the Grantors wanted to state this point explicitly because of the possibility that the Grantee might acquire other adjoining property and increase the burden on the Easement Area.

whatsoever, except that if Grantee damages the driveway through negligence or extraordinary use of the driveway, then Grantee will repair the damage at Grantee's expense.[4]

4. Improvements; Removal of Obstructions; Access. Either party may lay down a gravel or rock driveway within the Easement Area, up to eight feet wide, to provide a roadway for vehicles using the Easement Area.[5] Either party may remove trees and natural obstructions within the Easement Area at that party's expense. The party that removes trees or other natural obstructions will be responsible for obtaining any necessary governmental permits for the work. Grantors shall not construct, or permit the construction of, any building, improvement, or structure upon the Easement Area that would block Grantee's use of the Easement Area. This does not impose any duty on Grantors to remove natural vegetation from the Easement Area or to repair any damage resulting from natural causes.[6]

5. Binding Effect. This Agreement, and the rights and obligations herein, run with the land and bind and benefit future owners of the Grantor Tract and the Grantee Tract. This Agreement is intended to create a covenant running with the land.

6. No Dedication. This Agreement shall not be interpreted or construed to create any third-party beneficiary rights in any person other than the Grantors, the Grantee, and their respective successors and assigns with respect to the fee ownership of the Grantor Tract and the Grantee Tract, and any subdivision or parcel thereof. This Agreement shall not be deemed a gift or dedication of the Easement Area or any other portion of any property to any governmental agency, to any private third party, or to the general public whatsoever.[7]

7. Attorneys' Fees. In the event suit or action is instituted to interpret, enforce, or rescind this Agreement, the prevailing party shall be entitled to recover from the other party such sum as the court may adjudge reasonable as attorneys' fees.

---

[4] The agreement includes this unusual clause because the Grantors were willing to allow the Grantee to have access to build a house and use the Grantee Tract for recreation, but not to take on any maintenance obligation. The Grantors' driveway connected to a public street, "Garrideb Road." The Grantors wanted to maintain their driveway however they wished and not to be obligated to keep it up to any certain standard. If the parties want to maintain the road to a higher standard, the drafter should include a statement that allocates the cost to maintain the road, whether it is to be in equal shares or in accordance with the length that each uses, or as set by statute.

[5] The Easement Area is wider than 8 feet because it will need to accommodate utilities when the Grantee builds a house on the Grantee Tract. The parties wanted to strictly limit the width of the driveway so that it would retain its character as a driveway and not appear to be a private or public street. Neither the Grantors nor the Grantee wanted the driveway to be paved. The drafter would not include this restriction to a gravel surface if the properties were in a jurisdiction that required all driveways to be paved.

[6] The Grantors were willing to allow the Grantee to clear trees and brush from the driveway area when the Grantee was ready to build, but didn't want to take on the task of cutting trees and brush for themselves.

[7] I like to include this language in access easements as evidence that neither party is intending to create any rights in the public. I thought this language especially important here for two reasons. First is that the driveway physically looks like an extension of the dead-end "Garrideb Road." Second is that in the actual circumstance, an obscure public agency had a limited right to use the driveway for access to an unstaffed drainage facility. The actual agreement on which this form is based included several paragraphs that described the agency's use of the driveway, identified the specific easement agreement under which the agency was using the driveway, and disclaimed any intention to dedicate the road to the public.

8. Modifications. Any modifications to this Agreement must be in writing and signed by the Parties, or by their respective heirs, successors, or assigns.

9. Governing Law. This Agreement is made under Oregon law.

10. Severability. Any provision of this Agreement which is found to be invalid or in violation of any statute, rule, regulation, or common law shall be considered null and void, with the remaining provisions remaining in effect.

11. Entire Agreement. This Agreement constitutes the entire agreement of the Parties with respect to the Easement Area. This Agreement supersedes and replaces all written and oral agreements previously made or existing between the Parties.

GRANTORS: GRANTEE:

______________________________ ______________________________

____

[Insert signature and notarization blocks here]

Exhibit A: Legal Description of Grantor Tract
Exhibit B: Legal Description of Grantee Tract
Exhibit C: Depiction of Easement Area
Exhibit D: Legal Description of Easement Area

Easement Maintenance Agreement

Author's note: This easement agreement incorporates several concepts from the book. First, it's an access easement for a group of neighbors who share a private road, "Fillmore Lane," to use the private road to get to a nearby public street, "Chester Avenue." Second, it provides for the use of an existing bridge that's on the property of one of the parties, meaning that it provides a legal framework for the parties to use an existing encroachment. Third, it allocates maintenance responsibility based on the number of houses—vacant lots don't have to contribute.

EASEMENT MAINTENANCE AGREEMENT

PARTIES:

WHEELER, William A. and Mary K.
[Address]

WILSON, Henry and Harriet
[Address]

HENDRICKS, Eliza
[Address]

MORTON, Levi P. and Anna L.
[Address]

BRECKINRIDGE, John C. and Mary B.
[Address]

JOHNSON, Richard M.
CHINN, Julia
[Address]

EASEMENT MAINTENANCE AGREEMENT

This EASEMENT MAINTENANCE AGREEMENT is made as of _____________, 2020, by and among WILLIAM A. WHEELER and MARY K. WHEELER, as trustees of the William and Mary Wheeler Trust U/D/T June 12, 2013 (together "**Wheeler**"); HENRY WILSON and HARRIET WILSON (together, "**Wilson**"); ELIZA HENDRICKS ("**Hendricks**"); LEVI P. MORTON and ANNA L. MORTON (together "**Morton**"); JOHN C. BRECKINRIDGE and MARY B. BRECKINRIDGE (together "**Breckinridge**"); and RICHARD M. JOHNSON and JULIA CHINN (together "**Johnson-Chinn**"). These parties are collectively referred to as the "**Parties**."[1]

---

[1] The names of the parties are drawn from American history of the mid-nineteenth century.

RECITALS

A. Wheeler owns certain real property in Cayuga County, Oregon, with Property Identification number R123456, legally described in **Exhibit A** (the "**Wheeler Property**"). The Wheeler Property is a vacant lot.

B. Wilson owns two parcels of real property in Cayuga County, Oregon, at 1800 SE Fillmore Lane, Moravia, Oregon, with Property Identification numbers R234567 and R345678,[2] legally described in **Exhibit B** (the **"Wilson Properties"**). The Wilson Properties are near to and generally northeast of the Wheeler Property.

C. Hendricks owns certain real property in Cayuga County, Oregon, at 1804 SE Fillmore Lane, Moravia, Oregon, legally described in **Exhibit C** (the "**Hendricks Property**"). The Hendricks Property is adjacent to and generally northeast of the Wheeler Property.

D. Morton owns certain real property in Cayuga County, Oregon, at 1808 SE Fillmore Lane, Moravia, OR 97080, legally described in **Exhibit D** (the "**Morton Property**"). The Morton Property is adjacent to and generally east of the Wheeler Property.

E. Breckinridge owns certain real property in Cayuga County, Oregon, at 1812 SE Fillmore Lane, Moravia, Oregon, legally described in **Exhibit E** (the "**Breckinridge Property**"). The Breckinridge Property is near to and generally east of the Wheeler Property.

F. Johnson-Chinn owns certain real property in Cayuga County, Oregon, at 1816 SE Fillmore Lane, Moravia, Oregon, legally described in **Exhibit F** (the "**Johnson-Chinn Property**"). The Johnson-Chinn Property is partially adjacent to and generally southeast of the Wheeler Property.

G. Wilson, Hendricks, Morton, Breckinridge, and Johnson-Chinn (together the "**Residential Parties**") each own a residential building on their respective properties (together the "**Residential Properties**").

H. For many years the Residential Parties have accessed the Residential Properties by way of a paved portion of SE Fillmore Lane[3] (the **"Driveway"**) that crosses a bridge over Arthur Creek (the **"Bridge"**) and connects to SE Chester Avenue. The Bridge and portions of the Driveway are located on the Wheeler Property. The Bridge is on the portion of the Wheeler Property legally described in **Exhibit G** (the "**Bridge Area**"). The Driveway is on the portion of the Wheeler Property legally described in **Exhibit H** (the "**Driveway Area**").[4] The Bridge Area and the Driveway Area are depicted on the attached **Exhibit I**.

---

[2] This agreement contemplates that, in the future, each of the Wilson Properties may have its own house. The reason for identifying both parcels is to be clear that both parcels are independent benefited properties.

[3] In this example, "Fillmore Lane" (a pseudonym) is a private road. "Chester Avenue" (also a pseudonym) is a public street. The houses all use the private road to get from Chester Avenue to their individual driveways and garages.

[4] Use the recitals in your easement agreement to tell the story behind why the parties are making the agreement and the facts that are relevant to their agreement.

I. Wheeler desires to grant an easement allowing the Residential Parties to continue to use the Bridge Area and the Driveway Area for the purpose of ingress and egress to and from the Residential Properties.

J. This Easement Maintenance Agreement is not intended to, and does not limit, alter, remove, or expand any other easements on the Parties' properties.[5]

NOW, THEREFORE, for good and valuable consideration, the receipt and adequacy of which are hereby acknowledged, the parties agree as follows:

1. Wheeler hereby grants to the Residential Parties the nonexclusive right to use the Bridge Area and the Driveway Area (together the "**Easement Area**") for the purpose only of vehicular and pedestrian access to and from the Residential Properties (the **"Easement"**). The sole purpose of this Easement is to provide access to and from the Residential Properties on a portion of the Wheeler Property.

2. Wheeler expressly reserves the right to the free and unrestricted use (including paving and other construction) of the Easement Area, provided that any use shall not include construction of a building in the Easement Area or otherwise restrict access to the Residential Properties.[6]

3. The parties agree that their rights and obligations relating to the Easement Area shall be governed by ORS 105.170 *et seq.*, as it may be amended from time to time. The Residential Parties use the Easement Area at the Residential Parties' own risk and release Wheeler from any liability for injury to the Residential Parties and damage to the Residential Properties and the Residential Parties' personal property resulting in any way from the Residential Parties' use of the Easement Area.

4. The Parties agree that the Parties' use of the Easement Area shall be limited to reasonable residential use for the purpose of ingress and egress to and from the Parties' properties. The Parties' use shall not pollute the Easement Area, or the property adjacent to the Easement Area.

5. The Parties shall maintain the Driveway Area, the Bridge Area, and the Bridge to be safe and reasonably flat and readily passable by pedestrians and small cars.[7] The costs and expenses of

---

[5] If you state at the end of your easement agreement that "This Agreement is the complete agreement between the parties and replaces all prior agreements and understandings" without verifying that the parties don't have any other agreements and understandings, then you may inadvertently do away with agreements that are important to the parties. This agreement is based on a situation where the common driveway crossed the parcels of several of the parties, some of whom had recorded easements to use parts of the driveway and some of whom didn't. I did not want to imply that this agreement, which included all the users of the driveway, replaced any of the individual easements that some of them might have for the driveway and for utility lines.

[6] "Wheeler," who owned the portion of the private road covered by this agreement, wanted to reserve the right to widen the road on the Wheeler property without submitting those improvements to a vote of the other owners under paragraph 5.

[7] Why "pedestrians and small cars" instead of the broader "vehicular and pedestrian access" that appears in paragraph 1? The parties had two reasons for limiting the maintenance standard to be for pedestrians and small cars. The first reason was that the private road passed through several other parcels, and none of the owners wanted to give any of the other owners the right to widen the private road on anyone else's property without the consent of a majority of the owners. The second reason was that the parties did not want to be forced to upgrade the bridge to accommodate truck traffic or be usable by anyone who might want to store heavy equipment on their property.

maintaining and improving the Driveway Area, the Bridge Area, and the Bridge shall be allocated on a pro-rata basis among the Parties according to each party's number of **Shares**. Each party shall have one Share for each parcel of real property that party owns that contains a residential or commercial building. Each party with at least one share shall be called a **Shareholder**. A majority vote of the Shareholders is required before any proposed improvement or maintenance of the Driveway Area, the Bridge Area, or the Bridge can occur.

6. In any litigation between the Parties with respect to this Easement Maintenance Agreement, the prevailing party shall be entitled to recover, in addition to all other sums and relief, its reasonable attorney fees incurred both at and in preparation for arbitration, trial and any appeal or review, the amount to be set by the arbitrator(s) or court(s) before which the matter is heard.

7. The easement granted hereunder is appurtenant to and runs with the Wheeler Property and the Residential Properties, including any division or partition of any property.[8] The rights, easements, covenants, liabilities and obligations contained in this Easement Maintenance Agreement shall bind, burden and benefit each party's successors and assigns, lessees, mortgagees, and beneficiaries of a deed of trust.

[Insert the signature lines and notarizations here.]

Exhibit A: Legal Description of the Wheeler Property

Exhibit B: Legal Description of the Wilson Properties

Exhibit C: Legal Description of the Hendricks Property

Exhibit D: Legal Description of the Morton Property

Exhibit E: Legal Description of the Breckinridge Property

Exhibit F: Legal Description of the Johnson-Chinn Property

Exhibit G: Legal Description of the Bridge Area

Exhibit H: Legal Description of the Driveway Area

Exhibit I: Depiction of the Bridge Area and the Driveway Area

---

[8] Because the properties were located between a stream and a steep hillside, the parties were all very confident that the site would not become useful for commercial purposes or for high-density development. However, no one wanted to give up the right to partition their property into two or three parcels.

Reciprocal Easement Agreement

Author's Note: The owners of two large adjoining tracts shared the south 100+ feet of a common driveway that then forked to their separate houses. The common portion of the driveway meandered from one parcel to the other. Bits of one of the separate driveways were on the other parcel. The neighbors intended this agreement to allow them to continue to use their driveways as they and their predecessors had been doing for decades, and to allow each of them to eventually sell their properties without having to state that they had no agreement to use the common driveway.

RECIPROCAL EASEMENT AGREEMENT

PARTIES: GLADSTONE, William E. and Catherine G.
[Address]

GASCOYNE-CECIL, Robert A. and Georgina A.
[Address]

Affects tax parcels: ____________ and ____________

After Recording Return To:
Dean N. Alterman
Alterman Law Group PC
805 SW Broadway, Suite 1580
Portland, OR 97205

RECIPROCAL EASEMENT AGREEMENT

This RECIPROCAL EASEMENT AGREEMENT is made as of January 5, 2020 by and between WILLIAM E. GLADSTONE and CATHERINE G. GLADSTONE (together "**Gladstone**"), whose address is ________________________, and ROBERT A. GASCOYNE-CECIL and GEORGINA A. GASCOYNE-CECIL, as trustees of the Gascoyne-Cecil Family Trust under agreement dated August 22, 2003 (together and as trustees "**Gascoyne-Cecil**"), whose address is ____________________.

RECITALS

A. Gladstone owns the certain real property in Beaconsfield County, Oregon, at ____________________, legally described in **Exhibit A** (the "**Gladstone Property**").

B. Gascoyne-Cecil owns the certain real property in Beaconsfield County, Oregon, at ____________________, legally described in **Exhibit B** (the **"Gascoyne-Cecil Property"**). The Gascoyne-Cecil Property is partially adjacent to and generally west of the Gladstone Property.

C. For many years Gladstone has had a gravel driveway (the **"Driveway"**) generally following the westernmost property line of the Gladstone Property from the southern property line to the house located on the Gladstone Property.

D. In 2013, Gascoyne-Cecil discovered that a small portion of the Driveway encroaches o the Gascoyne-Cecil Property.

E. The parties desire to grant reciprocal easements allowing for Gladstone to continue to us that portion of the Gascoyne-Cecil Property shown on the attached **Exhibit C** as the **"Encroachmen Area"** as a gravel driveway, and allowing for Gascoyne-Cecil to use that portion of the Driveway show on the attached **Exhibit C** as the **"Shared Driveway Area"** for the purpose of ingress and egress to an from the Gascoyne-Cecil Property.[1]

NOW, THEREFORE, for good and valuable consideration, the receipt and adequacy of which ar hereby acknowledged, the parties agree as follows:

The Driveway Easement

1. Gladstone hereby grants to Gascoyne-Cecil the nonexclusive right to use the Share Driveway Area for the purpose only of vehicular and pedestrian access to and from the Gascoyne-Ceci Property (the **"Driveway Easement"**). This Driveway Easement does not authorize Gascoyne-Cecil t construct any improvements in or above or underneath the Shared Driveway Area. This Reciproca Easement Agreement does not authorize Gascoyne-Cecil to construct, install, or maintain any utility line in the Shared Driveway Area. The sole purpose of this Driveway Easement is to provide access to an from the Gascoyne-Cecil Property on a portion of Gladstone's existing Driveway.

2. Gladstone expressly reserves the right to the free and unrestricted use (including pavin and other construction)[2] of the Shared Driveway Area, provided that any use shall not includ construction of a building in the Shared Driveway Area or otherwise restrict access to the Gascoyne-Ceci Property.

3. The parties agree that their rights and obligations relating to the Shared Driveway Are shall be governed by ORS 105.170 *et seq.*, as it may be amended from time to time. Gascoyne-Cecil use the Shared Driveway Area at Gascoyne-Cecil's own risk and releases Gladstone from any liability fo injury to Gascoyne-Cecil and damage to the Gascoyne-Cecil Property and Gascoyne-Cecil's persona property resulting in any way from Gascoyne-Cecil's use of the Encroachment Area.

The Encroachment Easement

4. Gascoyne-Cecil hereby grants to Gladstone the nonexclusive right to use th Encroachment Area for the purpose only of maintaining the Driveway (the **"Encroachment Easement"** This Encroachment Easement does not authorize Gladstone to construct any improvements in or above o underneath the Encroachment Area. This Reciprocal Easement Agreement does not authorize Gladston

---

[1] The parties had obtained a survey that showed the encroachments in relation to the houses on the property and th property line, but had not obtained an exact legal description of the parts of the driveway that encroached onto on parcel or the other. As a result, they could identify the easement area only through the diagram that the surveyor ha provided.

[2] Gladstone reserved the right to pave the portion of the shared driveway on the Gladstone property, and did nc want Gascoyne-Cecil to have the right to pave Gladstone's property. Note that Recital E refers to the grave driveway and does not imply that Gascoyne-Cecil can pave Gladstone's part of the driveway.

to construct, install, or maintain any utility lines in the Encroachment Area. The sole purpose of this Encroachment Easement is to allow Gladstone to maintain the Encroachment Area as the Driveway.

5. Gascoyne-Cecil expressly reserves the right to the free and unrestricted use (including paving and other construction) of the Encroachment Area, provided that any use shall not include construction of a building in the Encroachment Area or otherwise prevent the use of the Encroachment Area as a Driveway.

6. The parties agree that their rights and obligations relating to the Encroachment Area shall be governed by ORS 105.170 *et seq.*, as it may be amended from time to time. Gladstone uses the Encroachment Area at Gladstone's own risk and releases Gascoyne-Cecil from any liability for injury to Gladstone and damage to the Gladstone Property and Gladstone's personal property resulting in any way from Gladstone's use of the Encroachment Area.

Miscellaneous Provisions

7. The parties agree that the parties' use of the Encroachment Area and the Shared Driveway Area shall be limited to reasonable residential[3] use for the purpose of ingress and egress to and from the parties' properties. The parties' use shall not pollute the Encroachment Area, the Shared Driveway Area, or the property adjacent to the Encroachment Area and Shared Driveway Area.

8. The parties shall maintain the Encroachment Area and the Shared Driveway Area to be reasonably flat and readily passable by pedestrians and small cars. This Reciprocal Easement Agreement does not give any party the right to require that the Encroachment Area and the Shared Driveway Area be paved. If Gascoyne-Cecil builds a second house on the Gascoyne-Cecil Property and begins using the Shared Driveway Area for ingress and egress to the Gascoyne-Cecil Property, the parties will divide the expense of maintenance of the Shared Driveway Area and Encroachment Area as follows:

Owner	Percentage
Gascoyne-Cecil	50%
Gladstone	50%

9. Gascoyne-Cecil and Gladstone agree that no party shall use herbicides or pesticides within twenty (20) feet of the Encroachment Area, the Shared Driveway Area, and the property line between the Gladstone Property and the Gascoyne-Cecil Property.[4]

10. In any litigation between the parties with respect to this Reciprocal Easement Agreement, the prevailing party shall be entitled to recover, in addition to all other sums and relief, its reasonable attorney fees incurred both at and in preparation for arbitration, trial and any appeal or review, the amount to be set by the arbitrator(s) or court(s) before which the matter is heard.

11. The easements granted hereunder are appurtenant to and run with the Gladstone Property and the Gascoyne-Cecil Property, including any division or partition of any property. The rights,

[3] The parties did not want the driveway to be used for any non-residential purpose.

[4] Each party was considering applying to certify the farm portion of their property as an organic farm, and did not want the other party's pesticides to disqualify them.

easements, covenants, liabilities and obligations contained in this Reciprocal Easement Agreement shal bind, burden and benefit each party's successors and assigns, lessees, mortgagees (or beneficiaries in a deed of trust).

IN WITNESS WHEREOF, this Reciprocal Easement Agreement has been executed effective a of the date first above written.

[Insert signature blocks and notarizations here.]

Exhibits:

Exhibit A	Legal Description of Gladstone Property
Exhibit B	Legal Description of Gascoyne-Cecil Property
Exhibit C	Depiction of the Encroachment Area and Shared Driveway Area

Utility Easement Agreement

Author's note: This easement agreement is a utility easement appurtenant to two parcels owned by the same grantee. The grantors each own half of a common driveway, over which the grantee had access rights but no utility rights. The purpose of this agreement is to give the grantee the right to run utility lines in the common driveway and out to "Manhattan Avenue." Unlike most utility easements granted to a service provider, this easement is appurtenant to the two grantee tracts and is not an easement in gross.

UTILITY EASEMENT AGREEMENT

Grantor: MAGUIRE, Michelle
[Address]

TRAVIS, James
[Address]

Grantee: HUNTER, Richard
[Address]

Affects: [Insert parcel numbers here]

After recording return to:
[Name and Address]

==================================

UTILITY EASEMENT AGREEMENT

This Utility Easement Agreement (this "Agreement") is made as of July ____, 2018 by and between MICHELLE MAGUIRE ("Maguire") and JAMES TRAVIS ("Travis") (Maguire and Travis together the "Grantors"), as grantors, and RICHARD HUNTER ("Grantee"), as grantee, in connection with properties in Alger County, Oregon owned by Grantors and Grantee.

RECITALS

A. Grantee owns two tax lots in the City of Horatio, Alger County, Oregon, commonly known as 1868 Manhattan Avenue, legally described on the attached **Exhibit 1** ("**Grantee Tract 1**"), and as 1870 Manhattan Avenue, legally described on the attached **Exhibit 2** ("**Grantee Tract 2**"). The term "**Grantee Tracts**" means Grantee Tract 1 and Grantee Tract 2.

B. Travis owns real property in the City of Horatio, Alger County, Oregon, commonly known as 1880 Manhattan Avenue and legally described on the attached **Exhibit 3** ("**Travis Tract**").

C. Maguire owns real property in the City of Horatio, Alger County, Oregon, commonly known as 1890 Manhattan Avenue and legally described on the attached **Exhibit 4** ("**Maguire Tract**").

D. The Grantee Tracts are immediately west of the Travis Tract, and immediately north of the portion of the Travis Tract extending to Manhattan Avenue. The Travis Tract is immediately west of the Maguire Tract, and immediately north of the portion of the Maguire Tract extending to Manhattan Avenue.

E. The Travis Tract and the Maguire Tract have access from Manhattan Avenue by a private drive (the "**Private Drive**"), wherein Travis owns the northern portion of the Private Drive and Maguire owns the southern portion of the Private Drive. The property map is depicted on the attached **Exhibit 5.**[1]

F. Grantee wishes to obtain an easement across the Private Drive for utilities purposes for the benefit of each of Grantee Tract 1 and Grantee Tract 2.

G. Travis and Maguire each wish to grant Grantee a nonexclusive easement across the Private Drive so that Grantee may extend utility lines to each of Grantee Tract 1 and Grantee Tract 2.

H. In consideration of the value received by Travis and Maguire, Travis and Maguire are each willing to grant the easement described in this Agreement, on the terms and conditions set forth in this Agreement.

THE PARTIES AGREE:

1. Grant of Easement. For good and valuable consideration, Travis and Maguire each grant to Grantee, its successors, and its assigns, a non-exclusive perpetual utility easement over and across a portion of the Private Drive, not to exceed 10 feet in width,[2] for the maintenance, operation, repair, and replacement of underground utility lines and related surface markers, conduits, lines, and facilities, as approximately depicted on the attached **Exhibit 6** ("**Utility Easement Area**"). This Easement benefits and is appurtenant to each of Grantee Tract 1 and Grantee Tract 2 individually.

2. Maintenance. Grantee will maintain, repair, and replace when necessary those utilities within the Utility Easement Area that serve the Grantee Tracts exclusively. The cost to

[1] I almost always describe how the properties lie in relation to one another so that fifty years from now a reader can work out the purpose of the easement, even if later owners have adjusted property lines, combined parcels, or lost bits to condemnation.

[2] I didn't specify the exact location of the Utility Easement Area because the actual lines are going to be installed not by Hunter (the grantee) but by the utility companies that will provide the services, who will choose locations that are compatible with the existing utilities in the easement area. I did limit where the Utility Easement Area could be when I stated that it must be within the Private Drive. The two Grantor Tracts are flag lots, each with a twenty-foot-wide "flagpole" portion running to the public street. The Private Drive runs east from the public street along the flagpole portions of the two lots, with each grantor owning half of the Private Drive.

maintain, repair, and replace utilities that serve the tracts of more than one party will be shared by the owners of those tracts, with each tract paying an equal share of the cost.[3] The parties shall maintain the Utility Easement Area and underlying utilities in good and safe operating condition and repair. The Parties shall cause all work on the Utility Easement Area to be done in a lien-free, good, and workmanlike manner and in compliance with applicable law.

3. **Notice; Restoration.** Grantee shall give seven days' notice to Travis and Maguire before disturbing the surface of the Utility Easement Area,[4] or in case emergency repairs are needed such shorter notice as is reasonable under the circumstances. Grantee shall restore the Utility Easement Area disturbed by the Grantee to a condition equivalent to, or better than, that which existed prior to the disturbance.

4. **Relocation Right.** Travis and Maguire collectively reserve the right, upon notice to Grantee, and at no expense to Grantee, to relocate all or any part of the Utility Easement Area and the utilities within the Utility Easement Area to another area on or off of Travis's or Maguire's properties,[5] as Travis and Maguire may determine together. If Travis and Maguire relocate all or part of the Utility Easement Area and underlying utilities, Travis and Maguire shall (i) provide a reasonable area for the relocated utilities substantially in the same width as the Utility Easement Area relocated; (ii) construct the utilities in the relocated Utility Easement Area of comparable capacity, function, size, and quality to those then installed and operated in the Utility Easement Area being relocated and vacated; and (iii) connect the relocated utilities to the termini of the utilities feeding to and flowing from the relocated utilities at the boundaries of the relocated Utility Easement Area. Grantee shall reasonably cooperate and coordinate with the party performing the relocation with respect to any relocation proposed by that party so as to avoid unreasonable interference with use of the Utility Easement Area. If Travis and Maguire together[6] exercise this right of relocation, either Travis or Maguire shall provide Grantee with a written notice setting forth the description of the relocated Utility Easement Area ("**Relocated Easement Description**") and notice of their election to relocate the Utility Easement Area or any portion thereof. Upon notice to Grantee, completion of the relocated Utility Easement Area and underlying utilities, and the recording of a supplement to this Agreement, referring to this Agreement in reasonable detail and setting forth the Relocated Easement Description, the

[3] This agreement is unusual in that the two grantors each own one tract and the grantee owns two tracts. If you simply say that the parties will share the cost of common lines "equally," do you mean that Travis, Maguire, and Hunter will each pay one-third, or that the owner of each of the four tracts will pay one-quarter? When you've drafted your cost-sharing provisions, read them a second or third time and rewrite anything that might be ambiguous.

[4] You can require the grantee to give the grantors reasonable notice before the grantee constructs or repairs utility lines, both because it's reasonable for a property owner to want advance notice before the easement holder enters to do work, and in this instance because the easement area is part of a common private driveway, and the work will interfere with access to the grantors' tracts.

[5] This is an easement for utility services and not for access. The grantee doesn't much care how the power and water connections get to the Grantee Tracts. If the grantors should obtain an easement across other nearby property to provide utility connections to the Grantee Tracts, the grantee is willing to let the grantors move the lines if the grantors pay the cost to move them.

[6] I represented the grantee. I did not want the grantee's lines to be moved unless both grantors agreed on where to move them.

Relocated Easement Description automatically shall replace and supersede the prior description of the Utility Easement Area affected by the relocation. From and after the completion of the work and the recording of the Relocated Easement Description, Grantee shall have no further right or interest in or to the prior Utility Easement Area that was relocated as provided above, or any underlying utilities in the Utility Easement Area that were relocated by Travis and Maguire. Notwithstanding and without diminishing the unilateral and self-executing nature of the foregoing right of Travis and Maguire together to relocate the Utility Easement Area from time to time, Grantee, upon demand from and without cost to the relocating party, shall execute, acknowledge, and deliver to that party any agreement as that party shall reasonably require to evidence the relocation of the Utility Easement Area as provided in this section.

5. **Non-Exclusivity.** Travis and Maguire each reserve the right to use and improve, and to allow third parties to use, their respective portions of the Utility Easement Area at any time, in any manner, and for any purpose that does not unreasonably interfere with the utilities in the Utility Easement Area that serve either Grantee Tract 1 or Grantee Tract 2.

6. **Easement Appurtenant.** This Agreement and the easements created by this Agreement run with the land and bind and benefit future owners of Grantee Tract 1, Grantee Tract 2, the Travis Tract, and the Maguire Tract.

7. **Modification/Termination.** This Agreement and the easements created by this Agreement can be modified only by written and recorded amendment signed by the owners of Grantee Tract 1, Grantee Tract 2, the Travis Tract, and the Maguire Tract.

8. **Attorneys' Fees.** In any litigation between the parties with respect to this Agreement, the prevailing party shall be entitled to recover, in addition to all other sums and relief, its reasonable attorneys' fees incurred both at and in preparation for arbitration, trial, and any appeal or review, the amount to be set by the arbitrator(s) or court(s) before which the matter is heard.

9. **Governing Law.** This Agreement shall be construed and enforced in accordance with the laws of the State of Oregon.

10. **Severability.** Any provision of this Agreement which is found to be invalid or in violation of any statute, rule, regulation, or common law shall be considered null and void, with the remaining provisions remaining in effect.

11. **Entire Agreement.** This Agreement constitutes the entire agreement of the Parties with respect to the Grantee's use of the [Private Drive and][7] Utility Easement Area. [This

[7] If this agreement covered the Grantee's use of the Private Drive for access, I would have included these words. The parties already had other agreements in place about the Private Drive. I did not want this agreement to replace those prior agreements.

Agreement supersedes and replaces all written and oral agreements previously made or existing between the Parties.][8]

12. Counterpart Copies. This Agreement may be signed in multiple or counterpart copies, with electronic or facsimile signatures, [or with signatures affixed by DocuSign or other electronic means,][9] which together form one agreement.

GRANTORS:	**GRANTEE:**
______________________________	______________________________
James Travis	Richard Hunter
______________________________	
Michelle Maguire	

[Insert the appropriate notarization blocks here.]

Exhibit 1 - Legal Description of Grantee Tract 1

Exhibit 2 - Legal Description of Grantee Tract 2

Exhibit 3 - Legal Description of Travis Tract

Exhibit 4 - Legal Description of Maguire Tract

Exhibit 5 - Property Map

Exhibit 6 - Utility Easement Area

---

[8] See the previous footnote. As an alternative, I might have written "This Agreement supersedes all prior agreements and understandings between Grantors and Grantee about Grantee's use of the Utility Easement Area for connecting the Grantee Tracts to utility services" to make it clear that this agreement doesn't replace the agreements between the two grantors or the agreements in place about using the Private Drive for access.

[9] If your state has enabling legislation for electronic signatures on real estate documents, and if your county clerk will record documents with electronic signatures, include this provision to allow the parties to sign electronically.

View Easement Agreement

Grantor: KIEF, Nathan and Celia
[Address]

Grantee: FRIEND, Jonas B. and Barbara Hall
[Address]

[Add "After recording return to" address and property information for indexing]
==============================

VIEW EASEMENT AGREEMENT

This View Easement Agreement (this "Agreement") is made as of June ___, 2022 by NATHAN KIEF and CELIA KIEF (together, "Grantors"), as grantors, and JONAS B. FRIEND and BARBARA HALL FRIEND (together, "Grantees"), as grantees, in connection with properties in Harrison County, Oregon owned by Grantors and Grantees.

RECITALS

A. Grantors own the following parcels (collectively, the "Grantor Tracts"):

(i) Lots 1, 2, and 3, Block 10, BLUEFORD BLOCKS, in the City of Sutton, Harrison County, Oregon (the "South Property");

(ii) Lots 4 and 5, Block 10, BLUEFORD BLOCKS, in the City of Sutton, Harrison County, Oregon (the "Middle Property"); and

(iii) Lots 6 and 7, Block 10, BLUEFORD BLOCKS, in the City of Sutton, Harrison County, Oregon (the "North Property").

B. Grantees own Block B, BLUEFORD BLOCKS in the City of Sutton, Harrison County, Oregon (the "Grantee Tract"). The Grantee Tract adjoins and is east of a public street known as Oceanfront Drive.

C. The Grantor Tracts adjoin and are on the west side of Oceanfront Drive, generally west of the Grantee Tract. The Grantor Tracts border the Pacific Ocean.

D. Grantees wish to acquire a permanent view easement over the Grantor Tracts for the benefit of the Grantee Tract to protect the view of the beach and Pacific Ocean from the Grantee Tract over the Grantor Tracts, through a building height restriction on the Grantor Tracts that limits the height of all structures on the Grantor Tracts to no more than approximately 15 feet above the existing grade of Oceanfront Drive where it runs between the Grantor Tracts and the Grantee Tract. Grantors are willing to grant such a view easement to Grantees for the benefit of the Grantee Tract and to consent to a height restriction for structures on the Grantor Tracts.

NOW, THEREFORE, GRANTORS AND GRANTEES AGREE:

1. Grant of View Easement. Grantors grant to Grantees a perpetual view easement over the portion of the Grantor Tracts at and above an elevation of 90.00 feet[1] (this portion hereinafter the "Easement Area"),[2] for the benefit of and appurtenant to the Grantee Tract.

2. Prohibition on Construction within the Easement Area. No owner of any of the Grantor Tracts[3] will construct or allow to be constructed within the Easement Area any structure, pole, antenna, roof, wall, or other obstruction of the view from the Grantee Tract, excepting only attached chimneys for interior fireplaces and furnaces. The word "structure" is used in its broadest sense and is intended to prohibit the construction of any artificial element within the Easement Area, excepting attached chimneys, regardless of whether the element is defined as a "structure" by the applicable building codes and zoning codes.

[If you want to be less restrictive on encroachments, you could write: "*** within the Easement Area any structure, roof, wall, or other obstruction of the view from the Grantee Tract, excepting only flagpoles, antennae, and attached chimneys for interior fireplaces and furnaces."]

3. Prohibition on Two-Floor Houses. No owner of any of the House properties will construct or allow to be constructed a house or other structure on any of the House Properties that includes more than one floor at or above the grade of Oceanfront Drive.

4. Definition of "Elevation." The elevation of 90.00 feet above which no structure, pole, antenna, roof, wall, or other obstruction of the view from the Grantee Tract may be built or maintained on the Grantor Tracts is not necessarily an elevation with respect to sea level[4] and is figured with reference to the assumed elevations of the following existing improvements:

a. Floor level of the ground floor of the building on the Grantee Tract	89.66 feet[5]
b. Roof ridgeline of the house on the South Property	88.72 feet
c. Roof ridgeline of the house on the Middle Property	89.05 feet

---

[1] If you state an elevation for the lower limit of the area subject to the view easement, then state how you've figured that elevation. In this agreement, I define "elevation" in section 4.

[2] In agreements for access easements and utility easements, the Easement Area is a portion of the Grantor Tract that you can depict on an ordinary map or survey. In this agreement for a view easement, the Easement Area is the entirety of the Grantor Tracts, but only above a fixed elevation. It's still a good idea to attach a map that shows the relation of the Grantor Tracts to the Grantee Tract.

[3] I wrote this wording because the Grantors intended to sell the three Grantor Tracts over time to three different buyers.

[4] In this situation, the lower limit of the Easement Area was in fact about 90 feet above sea level. I did not want to fix the Easement Area in relation to sea level because sea level changes from time to time, sometimes because the government redefines "sea level" and sometimes because ground lifts or subsides. At the same time, I wanted to give future owners at least a rough idea of how high they could build by using several reference elevations that they could easily find.

[5] The Grantees had a surveyor measure all of these elevations as exactly as possible. The floor of the building and the roof ridgelines were all level, unlike Oceanfront Drive.

For reference, the elevation of 90.00 feet that marks the lower plane of the Easement Area is 15 feet above the current elevation of the lowest point of Oceanfront Drive where it adjoins the Grantor Tracts, plus or minus no more than 0.5 feet.[6]

5. **Binding Effect.** This Agreement and the easements created by this Agreement run with the land, bind future owners of the Grantor Tracts, collectively and individually, and benefit future owners of the Grantee Tract. This Agreement is intended to create a covenant running with the land for the exclusive benefit of the Grantee Tract. This Agreement is enforceable by the owner of the Grantee Tract against any infringing owner of any of the Grantor Tracts and is not enforceable by the owner of any of the Grantor Tracts against the owner of any of the other Grantor Tracts.[7]

6. **No Dedication.** This Agreement shall not be interpreted or construed to create any third-party beneficiary rights in any person other than Grantees and their successors and assigns with respect to the fee ownership of the Grantee Tract, and any subdivision or partition thereof. This Agreement does not convey or dedicate any right to the public or to any unit of government.

7. **Specific Performance.**[8] Grantors and Grantees are making this Agreement for the protection of the views of the beach and the Pacific Ocean from the Grantee Tract. Grantees shall have the right to seek and obtain a decree of specific performance to compel the owner of any Grantor Tract on which an obstruction is built or maintained within the Easement Area to remove the obstruction, if Grantees file suit within two years after the obstruction is built or maintained.[9] Grantees' failure to file suit to enjoin or remove any particular obstruction will not terminate Grantees' right to enforce this Agreement with respect to any other obstruction.

8. **Attorneys' Fees.** In the event suit or action is instituted to interpret, enforce, or rescind this Agreement, in addition to other relief that the court may grant, the prevailing party shall be entitled to recover from the other party such sum as the court may adjudge reasonable as attorneys' fees.

9. **Modifications.** Any modifications to this Agreement must be in writing and signed by the Parties, or by their respective heirs, successors, or assigns.

---

[6] The actual "Oceanfront Drive" is not quite level and has curbs and sidewalks that are several inches above the level of the driving lanes. I included the reference to the elevation of Oceanfront Drive so that future owners could calculate the lower plane of the Easement Area even if the buildings used as reference elevations were remodeled or demolished.

[7] The Grantor expected to sell the three Grantor Tracts to different buyers who would most likely remodel the houses on the Grantor Tracts, and did not want to give the three future buyers any right to limit the height of their neighbors' houses or to create the potential for litigation among the future buyers over the Easement Agreement.

[8] The Grantees are acquiring the view easement to protect their view of the ocean, which they can't replace with money damages.

[9] I included this provision to forestall the future owner of a Grantor Tract who started construction on a house that encroached into the Easement Area from arguing that the Grantees did not complain quickly enough—that is, that the Grantees should have complained when they saw the roof ridge being attached, or when they saw the walls being framed, or when they saw the foundation being poured.

10. Governing Law. This Agreement is made under Oregon law.

11. Severability. If any provision of this Agreement is held invalid, the other provisions will continue in effect. If any provision of this Agreement is held invalid as to one of the Grantee Tracts, the Agreement shall continue as a restriction on the other Grantee Tracts.

GRANTORS:	GRANTEES:
______________________________	______________________________
Nathan Kief	Jonas B. Friend
______________________________	______________________________
Celia Kief	Barbara Hall Friend

[Add notarizations]

EXHIBIT A

<u>Depiction of View Easement Area</u>

Landscaping Easement Agreement

Author's note: This agreement is an example of the "poor person's lot line adjustment," in which one neighbor gives to another the right to maintain landscaping up to an existing fence that does not follow the property line.

LANDSCAPING EASEMENT AGREEMENT

Grantor:	BRIDGEMAN, Charles [Address]
Grantees:	BROWN, Lancelot BROWN, Bridget Wayet [Address]

[Insert the "After recording return to" address and other information to identify the affected properties.]

===================================

LANDSCAPING EASEMENT AGREEMENT

This Landscaping Easement Agreement (this "Agreement") is made as of January ____, 2021 by CHARLES BRIDGEMAN ("Grantor"), as grantor,[1] and LANCELOT BROWN and BRIDGET WAYET BROWN ("Grantees"), as grantees.

RECITALS

A. Grantor owns property in Buckingham County, Oregon legally described on the attached Exhibit A (as so described, the "Grantor Tract"). The Grantor Tract is located in the Northwest and the Southwest quarter of Section 10, Township 6 South, Range 1 East of the Willamette Meridian.

B. Grantees own property in Buckingham County, Oregon legally described on the attached Exhibit B (as so described, the "Grantee Tract"). The Grantee Tract is adjacent to and south of the Grantor Tract.

C. A fence installed by Grantees' predecessors in interest some years ago near the property line common to the Grantor Tract and the Grantee Tract was recently surveyed and found to be north of the actual property line by a distance ranging from zero at the west end of the fence to approximately 25 feet at the east end of the fence. Grantor wishes to grant to Grantees a nonexclusive easement to maintain the fence in its current location, to landscape the

[1] I did not capitalize "grantor" here, nor "grantees" in the next line, because in these two instances I am using the words not as defined words but simply to describe what the parties are doing in this agreement.

portion of the Grantor Tract on the Grantees' side of the fence (the south side of the fence) while the fence is standing,[2] and to replace the fence with a similar fence when necessary.

NOW, THEREFORE, GRANTOR AND GRANTEES AGREE:

1. Grantor grants to Grantees a non-exclusive easement to maintain, repair, and replace[3] the fence within the area described on Exhibit C (the "Easement Area").[4] The Easement Area is depicted on Exhibit D.

2. Grantor grants to Grantees an easement to plant and maintain a lawn and shrubs (collectively, "landscaping"), but not trees,[5] in the Easement Area. Grantees do not have to plant any shrubs, but Grantees will maintain in good and attractive condition any shrubs that Grantees do plant and all grass and lawn within the Easement Area. Grantees will not construct or maintain any structure within the Easement Area except the present wood fence[, or a replacement of the present wood fence with a wood fence of similar construction and height].[6]

3. The easement[7] and the associated right to plant and maintain a lawn and landscaping on the Easement Area is perpetual [, but will terminate if the fence is demolished and the Grantees do not rebuild it within three months after the demolition. In that event, either party may construct a new fence on the property line between the Grantor Tract and the Grantee Tract, but the Grantees' right to use the Easement Area will terminate].[8]

---

[2] In the particular situation that resulted in this easement agreement, the grantor was willing to let the grantees landscape the area on the grantees' side of the fence as long as the fence was standing, but wanted to reserve the right to landscape it as the grantor wished if the grantees took the fence down and did not replace it.

[3] In this agreement, the neighbors are agreeing to treat the fence line as the effective property line indefinitely, which is why the agreement grants the Browns the right to replace the fence in the same location.

[4] I am defining "Easement Area" to be only that portion of the Grantor Tract that is south of the encroaching fence so that future readers of this agreement will not conclude that this agreement encumbers the entire Grantor Tract.

[5] Bridgeman may believe that trees that the Browns plant in the Easement Area will grow to block Bridgeman's view. Bridgeman can't prevent the Browns from planting trees on the Browns' property, but Bridgeman can decline to give the Browns permission to plant trees in the Easement Area.

[6] The bracketed language is Bridgeman giving the Browns the capability to replace the fence in the same location only if the Browns replace the fence with an equally attractive fence, but not if they want to replace the fence with a chain-link fence. If the parties want the easements to terminate if the fence is destroyed or demolished then they would omit this phrase.

[7] I use "easement" to mean the Grantees' right to use the Easement Area, and not to mean the agreement that creates the easement.

[8] Include the bracketed language if the grantor wants the easement rights to terminate if the fence is demolished without being replaced.

4. The easements created by this Agreement run with the land and bind and benefit future owners of the Grantor Tract and the Grantee Tract.

5. Grantor and Grantees acknowledge and agree that the east-west property line between the Grantor Tract and the Grantee Tract is the solid line of 363.30 feet as depicted on Exhibit D.[9]

GRANTOR:	GRANTEES:
______________________________	______________________________
Charles Bridgeman	Lancelot Brown
	______________________________
	Bridget Wayet Brown

Exhibits

Exhibit A:	**Legal Description of Grantor Tract (Bridgeman)**
Exhibit B:	**Legal Description of Grantee Tract (Brown)**
Exhibit C:	**Legal Description of the Easement Area**
Exhibit D:	**Depiction of the Easement Area**

[Attach acknowledgments in the proper form for your state.]

[9] Exhibit D is the surveyor's map, which indicates the property line between the Grantor Tract and the Grantee Tract as being 363.30 feet long. I included this sentence not only to help the reader identify which line on the map is the property line, but also to ward off a future claim for adverse possession. Disagreeable grantees may want to assert that they don't need an easement from the grantor because they or their predecessors have acquired title by adverse possession to the area on their side of the encroaching fence. If you include a sentence like this one, even in agreements with the kindliest and most Jekyll-like of grantees, then you are giving the grantor some protection against the litigious Hyde to whom the Jekylls may some day sell their property.

Exhibit A

Legal Description of Grantor Tract (Bridgeman)

[Here put the legal description of the entire Grantor Tract.]

Exhibit B

Legal Description of Grantee Tract (Brown)

[Here put the legal description of the entire Grantee Tract.]

Exhibit C

Legal Description of Fence and Landscaping Easement Area

[Here put the legal description of the Easement Area, which in this example could read something like this:

That portion of that certain tract conveyed to Charles Bridgeman by deed recorded on _________, 2014 at Book _____, Page ____, Buckingham County Records which lies south of the following-described line:

Beginning at the Southwest corner of the Bridgeman tract;

Thence North 86°14'00" East 369.22 feet to a point on the East line of the Bridgeman tract that is North 02°15'00" West of the Southeast corner of the Bridgeman tract.]

Exhibit D

Depiction of Easement Area

[Obtain a map from the parties' surveyor and insert it here.]

Acknowledgments

Even a book with the name of only one author on the cover is the result of the effort and experience of many. I gratefully appreciate the contributions of those whose ideas, support, and constructive criticism made it possible for me to write this book and for you to read it.

Those two sentences were true when I wrote them at the end of my first book for the American Bar Association, *How to Build a Real Estate Law Practice*, and they are true for this book as well.

I acquired much of the experience that I put into this book from thirty-two years of writing and interpreting easement agreements for my clients. I am grateful to each and every one of them for entrusting me with their work.

I appreciate the gentle advice of Alan Keiser of the Pennsylvania Bar, whose comments and suggestions led to many improvements from my manuscript to the finished product, the careful review and editing of Sylvia Rebert, Joanne Creary, and Shaina Lucas of Progressive Publishing Services, and the patience of Jeffrey Salyards of the American Bar Association, who edited this book and saw it through to publication.

Words flow easily from lawyers until they face a keyboard, and the actual writing took much longer than I'd expected. My law partner, Erica Menze of the Oregon and Washington Bars, never objected to the time that I took from our law practice to work on this book. Our small firm continued to thrive while I wrote, which is to her credit and that of our very able office administrator, Brittany Weld. I thank them both.

And, as with my other book, I express my gratitude to my wife, Susan T. Alterman of the Oregon and Washington Bars, for her time and thought in discussing many of these ideas with me, for suggesting topics to include, and for not begrudging the weekends that I sequestered myself to sit at my screen and type.

Index

Page numbers followed by "*f*" refer to figures. Page numbers followed by "n" refer to footnotes.

V

W

Z